WOMEN OF FAITH™
STUDY GUIDE SERIES

EXPERIENCING
SPIRITUAL
INTIMACY

BY

CHRISTA KINDE

FOREWORD BY

MARY GRAHAM

NELSON IMPACT
A Division of Thomas Nelson Publishers
Since 1798

www.thomasnelson.com

Published by Nelson Impact, a Division of Thomas Nelson, Inc., P.O. Box 141000, Nashville, Tennessee, 37214.

Scripture quotations marked NKJV are taken from *The Holy Bible*, The New King James Version (NKJV®). Copyright 1979, 1980, 1982, Thomas Nelson, Inc., Publishers. Used by permission. All rights reserved.

Scripture quotations marked NLT are taken from *The Holy Bible*, The New Living Translation (NLT). Copyright © 1986 by the Tyndale House Publishers, Wheaton, Illinois, 60189. Used by permission. All rights reserved.

Scripture quotations marked NCV are taken from *The Holy Bible*, New Century Version®. Copyright © 1987, 1988, 1991 by Word Publishing, a Division of Thomas Nelson, Inc. Used by permission. All rights reserved.

Scripture quotations marked MSG are taken from *The Holy Bible*, The Message (MSG). Copyright © 1993. Used by permission of NavPress Publishing Group. All rights reserved.

ISBN 1-4185-0709-1

06 07 08 EB 7 6 5 4 3 2 1

✦ Contents ✦

✦ FOREWORD ✦

Does God have a laptop? If so, I'd find it almost effortless early in the morning to connect with Him. The house is quiet (even the dog is sleeping!), the phone doesn't ring, and I'm not feeling pressed to move on to the next thing.

In fact, my favorite part of the day is in those wee hours when I sip coffee and have only my laptop for companionship. The world stops, no one is looking for me, and I'm not crazy-tired. If God had a laptop, that's when I'd write to Him and pour out my heart.

But since He has no laptop, I find other ways to meet and relate to Him in my innermost being. Quite honestly, intimacy of any kind doesn't come all that naturally to me. I grew up in a large, loud, laughing, story-telling family. No one had quiet time alone, time to think or reflect. In the first eighteen years of my life, I doubt I was ever by myself. And intimate conversations with someone? Not that I remember. No one made eye contact in conversation; no one really listened or expressed much empathy or tenderness to one another. We all talked at the same time, interrupted each other, and laughed hilariously at each other's stories. Fierce undying loyalty was our virtue—but intimacy? I don't think so.

When I came to Christ almost forty years ago, two things happened. First, I started forming friendships with people who walked with God, who prayed freely and openly about everything, and experienced intimacy with the Savior. I was intrigued and longed for that myself. Second, I began to notice that their ability for intimacy flowed over into other relationships as well. I observed real care expressed (more often than not, verbally) between believers. It was a skill I'd never learned, and one I mostly felt uncomfortable practicing, but I desired it nonetheless.

Admittedly, I've had to learn intimacy. If you want to exchange stories or discuss ideas with me, no problem. That comes easily to me. But intimacy is something I've had to intentionally choose to practice. Feeling comfortable in the presence of God with all of me—the good, bad, and ugly—is essential to my spiritual life. Knowing He knows everything about me and loves me anyway is crucial. And I've learned that feeling comfortable with that is heaven on earth.

When we "show up," He's there to meet us right where we are, to understand our needs and to invade our lives with His presence, love, grace, tender mercies, and direction. I find in the wee hours of the morning, as I sit with my Bible (and NOT my computer) open on my lap, I see the reality of verses like, "Be still, and know that I am God" (Psalms 46:10 NKJV). Or, "You have given him the joy of being in your presence" (Psalms 21:6 NLT). A Bible study that can take us there is an essential tool, whether we use it alone or in a small group of others who seek a real, life-changing connection with Him.

I'm grateful we have ways to connect intimately with God. I wouldn't want to email Him!

—Mary Graham

✦ INTRODUCTION ✦

Some of my favorite storylines are about a guy and two different women. The first gal is always the guy's best bud. They've known each other since forever. He's comfortable with her, tells her everything, trusts her completely. In return, she's loved him since forever, but he's never noticed. Then the second woman comes into the picture, and the guy is head over heels. In these stories the first gal is usually stuck in the position of confidant, comforter, and even messenger to the new lady love. But for love of her guy, she sets aside her own feelings and does what he asks of her. In the end, the guy's eyes are opened somehow and he sees his dear friend in a new light. Startled to find love so close at hand, he berates himself for never really seeing her before. And of course, they live happily ever after.

Many of us are blind to what is closest to us. In our hearts we long to experience spiritual intimacy. We want to know God and be known by Him. We long to see Jesus face to face, hear His voice, and touch His hand. We want to be close to God. We long to be His child, His beloved, His friend. We say we need a confidant and a comforter. Someone to trust and to tell our secrets to. We want God as our intimate—our close and personal friend. And in our yearning to be acknowledged by the Father and welcomed by the Son, we completely miss what is right in front of us. Or, what is right inside of us.

Do you know the treasure that is already hidden in your heart? Are you aware of the riches that are already yours? Those of us who are longing for spiritual intimacy need to have our eyes opened. The God we long to be close to is already closer than any sister, friend, or lover can come. God, the Holy Spirit, dwells in us. Do you long for spiritual intimacy? This study opens up your eyes to the Spirit's role in our lives. He knows us in intimate ways. Get to know Him!

*His Holy Spirit, moving and breathing in you, is the
most intimate part of your life, making you fit for himself.
Don't take such a gift for granted.*

Ephesians 4:30 MSG

CHAPTER 1

KNOWING GOD

"AND THIS IS ETERNAL LIFE, THAT THEY
MAY KNOW YOU, THE ONLY TRUE GOD, AND
JESUS CHRIST WHOM YOU HAVE SENT."

John 17:3 NKJV

Our family loves to go hiking. Nearly every weekend finds us packing up and heading out into the woods. Our favorite destination is a state-protected natural area surrounding a local lake. Trails of varying lengths and levels of difficulty wind through the trees, skirt small ponds, and zigzag up steep ridges. The first time we found this park, we were awed. Each bend in the trail brought us to some new and lovely scene. Now, the trails are becoming familiar. The more we revisit the paths, the more well-known each landmark becomes. A fallen tree covered with white mushrooms, a seven-trunked tree skirted with moss, a bench with a plaque reading, "Come aside and rest awhile." Each visit to the

CLEARING
✦ THE ✦
COBWEBS

Is there someplace you go to so regularly that you know it intimately— backward and forward?

forested hillsides has yielded new discoveries as well—violets in spring, a doe and her fawn, a snail shell, a turtle, a crawfish, a pretty rock.

As Christians, we talk about God as a personal God. He's *our* Father. He's *our* Lord. He's *our* Savior. One of the strongest desires of our hearts is to know God more. But getting to know God is much like hiking through the woods. What begins in awe-inspiring discovery becomes comfortably familiar over time. When we've walked with God for many years, there are landmarks we can point to—answered prayers, unexpected graces, needed comfort, and blessing upon blessing. And as we travel the trails in our spiritual lives, and they become well-worn and smooth with frequent use, we make new discoveries about God as well. We come to know God in personal ways.

1. God is big. Vast. Limitless. Infinite. Just as a hiker who sticks to the trails only gains a small glimpse of the vast woods she's traveling through, we can only begin to know our Heavenly Father. What does Job 36:26 say about our limitations in understanding of God?

I have learned that sometimes we will be aware of God's closeness and sometimes we won't. At times we experience the sweetness of God's nearness and at other times the frightening loneliness of His distance.

Patsy Clairmont

2. Despite the unsearchable nature of God, we begin with the assertion that God is God. It is a starting place for the relationship that will be built.

- **Exodus 8:10** – "That you may know that...

- **Deuteronomy 4:35** – "That you may know that...

- **Deuteronomy 4:39** – "Therefore know this day, and consider it in your heart, that...

- **Psalm 46:10** – "Be still, and know that...

- **Psalm 100:3** – "Know that...

3. What precious gift does God give to us, according to Jeremiah 24:7?

4. How does 1 John 5:19–20 say that we came to know God?

5. So how can we go about getting to know a God who is unknowable? What does Paul tell us in 1 Corinthians 2:10?

6. Let's read some more of this passage. According to 1 Corinthians 2:10–12, why have we received the Spirit of God in our hearts?

I know my own grocery store like the back of my hand. No matter what I might need, I know exactly where to find it. Yeast, raisins, popcorn, evaporated milk—I can quote you aisle and shelf. But drop me in the middle of a grocery store on the other side of town, and I might as well be in the Amazon forest. I've lost my sense of direction. I don't know how to navigate. I'm lost.

Getting to know God is often like getting to know a new grocery store. Just when we think we have God all figured out, something unexpected shakes us to our foundations. For a little while, we're lost. That's when we rely most on the Holy Spirit. He reminds us of the things that are unchanging, and helps us to readjust when God does the unexpected.

7. Has God ever surprised you, for better or for worse, and opened up your eyes to some new facet of Himself?

I need intimate contact with God. Our souls were made for this. When we deprive our souls of that very life force, we can survive—but that is all we are doing. We were not created to merely survive but to thrive in God.

Sheila Walsh

8. Getting to know God is a lifelong journey. We should never give up the pursuit. In Isaiah 58:2 we get a picture of what followers of God *should* be like. How are they characterized?

9. Each of us has some area in our life that we're proud of—some accomplishment, some talent, some characteristic, some facet of our personality. You might call it one of the reasons you're glad you're *you*! What does Jeremiah 9:24 say we should be proud of, boast about, or glory in?

DIGGING DEEPER

Do you think you can know God and not have it change your life? There are two sides to this. What is Paul's criticism of those who say they know God but don't show any evidence of it in Titus 1:16? And how does David describe a life lived in the pursuit of knowing God in 1 Chronicles 28:9? How has knowing God changed your life?

PONDER & PRAY

God is knowable, and we long to know Him intimately. This week as you ponder this, try to make a list of the ways in which God still "wows" you with awe-inspiring discoveries. Then add to that list the ways in which He has become a comfortable and familiar friend Are there landmarks in your relationship with Him? Thank the Lord this week for well-traveled trails you've shared with

Him, then ask God for new paths that will lead you to a more intimate knowledge of Him.

TRINKETS TO TREASURE

At the close of every Women of Faith conference, women are asked to play a little game of pretend. Each conference guest is asked to imagine that a gift has been placed in her hands—one from each of the speakers—to serve as reminders of the different lessons shared. This study guide will continue this tradition! At the close of each lesson, you will be presented with a small gift. Though imaginary, it will serve to remind you of the things you have learned. Think of it as a souvenir. Souvenirs are little trinkets we pick up on our journeys to remind us of where we have been. They keep us from forgetting the path we have traveled. Hide these little treasures in your heart, for as you ponder them, they will draw you closer to God.

TRINKET TO TREASURE

Your trinket this week—a walking stick—will serve as a reminder that our Christian walk gives us the chance to know God. Something to lean on as we travel the well-worn trails of God's continued goodness. A steadying handhold as we explore new paths with awe-inspiring vistas. A familiar accompaniment as we revisit the landmarks of our spiritual walk.

CHAPTER 2

BEING KNOWN

"NOW WHAT MORE CAN DAVID SAY TO YOU?
FOR YOU, LORD GOD, KNOW YOUR SERVANT."

2 Samuel 7:20 NKJV

y uncle is a total "cheese-head" (translation: Green Bay Packers fan). My Grandma loves the *The Cat Who...* mysteries by Lillian Jackson Braun. My husband has a thing for the Gold City quartet. I subscribe to all of Martha Stewart's magazines. (Did you know there are, like, four?) Have you ever been a fan of something or someone? Most of us have at some point or another. Or if we've not been fanatical ourselves, we know someone who has. You know what I mean. Never missing a new episode of your favorite television program. Knowing all the lyrics to all the songs of your favorite band. Tacking up posters of some teen heartthrob in your locker. Buying all

CLEARING
✦ THE ✦
COBWEBS

Is there anything or anyone that you could say you're a fan of?

their latest gadgets. Wearing their t-shirts. Getting season tickets. Buying their books. Going to their concerts. Tuning in to their daily radio program. Attending conventions. Whether it's Star Trek, Car Talk, or Crop Night, you're a fan.

The stereotypical fan gushes with enthusiasm, "I'm your biggest fan!" They prove their love by knowing everything they can about the object of their obsession. They're into the details—trivia, statistics, likes, lyrics. But every fan comes to the realization one day that their fascination is completely one-sided. They may know everything about their favorite author, actor, or performer, but to their idol, they are just another stranger.

1. To God, we're not just another face in the crowd. A real relationship is two-sided, and just as we are drawn to know all we can about God, God delights to know everything about us. What does Psalm 44:21 say that God knows about us?

I was in the God's mind before I was ever in the womb of my mother. Specific attention, thought, and planning took place about me before God actually formed me in the womb.

Marilyn Meberg

2. With most people, we can put on our best face. We can decide just how vulnerable we're willing to be. But according to 1 Samuel 16:7, when God looks at you, what does He see?

3. How is it that God knows us so well? What does Job 33:4 say He's done for each of us?

4. How does Job 10:8 describe our formation?

5. Our hearts long to be known intimately. God knew us before we ever took a breath! David celebrated God's intimate knowledge of his own beginnings. Take a look at Psalm 139:13–16 NKJV.

For You _____ my _____ _____; You _____ me in my mother's womb. I will praise You, for I am _____ and _____ made; Marvelous are Your works, And that my soul knows very well. My _____ was not _____ from You, When I was made in _____, And _____ wrought in the lowest parts of the earth. Your eyes saw my _____, being yet _____. And in Your book they all were written, The days _____ for me, When as yet there were none of them.

There's a chorus we often sing in our worship services at church. The lyrics in one of the verses go like this: "I see the stars that you have made. I know you call them each by name. To think Father God, whom heaven displays, is thinking of me in intimate ways." God is so big, and we are so small. Yet God cares about every little detail of our lives. He knows us intimately. He loves us unconditionally.

6. According to Ephesians 2:10, "God has made us what we are" (NCV). In other translations, what does that verse call us?

7. So if God knows us so well, what can we possibly have to say to him? What does 2 Samuel 7:20 tell us David said to the Lord?

8. David never stopped talking to God. What things did David say God knew about Himself in his Psalms?

    • Psalm 69:5

• Psalm 94:11

• Psalm 139:23

9. God knows us and loves us. How did He pour out that love into our lives, according to Romans 5:5?

DIGGING DEEPER

Usually, when we talk about God's all-knowing nature, we focus on the fact that He can see all the bad things we've ever done in secret. A good example of this can be found in Hebrews 4:13. Then, we discover that our not-so-secret-after-all sins are what separate us from God— effectively hiding Him from us. Look up Isaiah 59:2 for this point. Perhaps we need to take a page from David's book. He didn't avoid those little sins, figuring God knew they were there and that was enough. What did David willingly do, according to Psalm 32:5?

PONDER & PRAY

Our adoration of God is not one-sided. Even as we strive to know Him better, we can thrill to the fact that He knows us intimately. We needn't try to hide anything. We can tell Him anything. We'll never be misunderstood. What's more, it doesn't matter if words fail. He reads our emotions and interprets our silences. He just *knows* us! Thank God this week for the intimacy of His knowing.

TRINKET TO TREASURE

Just as fans yearn to know everything there is to know about the object of their affections, we are compelled to know God more and more. But while the average fan is just a face in the crowd and a stranger, we are recognized, known, and loved by our Lord. To remind us of this fact, our little gift this week is a pennant—the sort waved with excitement during sporting events. Though we wave it in the midst of a sea of cheering people, we are seen as individuals and known by God.

✦ Notes & Prayer Requests ✦

CHAPTER 3

I WILL SEND YOU A HELPER

"AND I WILL PRAY THE FATHER, AND HE WILL
GIVE YOU ANOTHER HELPER, THAT HE MAY
ABIDE WITH YOU FOREVER."

John 14:16 NKJV

Don't you just love side-kicks? They're always taking second billing. Mentioned more as an afterthought. A footnote in the life of their famous friend. Sidekicks rarely get as much attention as the main character, but you have to give them credit. They're always there. Outside the limelight, a sidekick is a hero's faithful friend, moral support, and right hand man. What would Lucy have done without Ethel? Where would the Lone Ranger be without Tonto? How could Fred Flintstone have managed without Barney Rubble? Could Frodo Baggins have finished his quest without Samwise Gamgee?

CLEARING ✦ THE ✦ COBWEBS

Did you have a nickname growing up?

Robinson Caruso had his man Friday. Don Quixote had Sancho Panza. Captain Kirk had Mr. Spock. Batman had Robin. Snoopy had Woodstock. Calvin had Hobbes. Yogi had Booboo. And Robin Hood had Little John. Even in the Bible, there were dynamic duos. Moses had Aaron. David had Jonathan. Paul had Barnabas. Aaron, Jonathan, and Barnabas didn't get the kind of admiration or attention that their friends received, but they were indispensable. Without them, the heroes of Scripture would have been very lonely. The heroes needed someone to listen. Someone to trust. Someone to understand. Someone to care. Someone to share their secrets. In the Lord's service, they needed a friend, a confidant, a helper.

We too cannot do the Lord's work alone. We need Someone to trust, to listen, to understand, to care. But our Helper is far superior to any earthly sidekick.

1. What did John the Baptizer say Jesus would do in Mark 1:8?

Jesus' desire is that His Word and His Spirit be our guides for life. Being a follower of Jesus Christ means becoming more and more like Him—letting His Spirit transform us into all we were created to be. That happens, dear friend, from the inside out.

Luci Swindoll

2. When the time came for Jesus to leave His disciples and return to His Father in Heaven, what news did He share to help comfort His friends?

3. Though we could hardly call Him a sidekick, God sent us the Helper we desperately needed. What did Jesus say the Helper would do in John 15:26?

4. What is another way in which this Spirit of truth could help believers, according to John 16:13?

5. What invaluable gift does the Spirit impart, according to John 14:26?

6. According to John 14:16, how long would this Helper stay with us?

*W*hen I was a kid, I always wanted a flashy nickname. My only nickname throughout my childhood had been rather uninspiring. Dad called me his Helper. Other kids had nicknames—Sport, Flicka, Gypsy, Red. One guy in my class had the ignominious middle name Howard, but was affectionately dubbed "Howie" throughout his high school years. I actually approached my parents on the subject, asking them if they could please give me a good nickname. My Dad explained that nicknames like that just kind of happen, and you can't invent them. So I was stuck with Helper.

It wasn't until much later that I took consolation from the fact that God Himself had that same nickname. God is called our Helper, and the Holy Spirit was sent to be a Helper. It may not be the flashiest nickname, but I'm in good company.

7. *Helper* may seem to be a humble term, but what does Psalm 54:4 tell us about the Lord?

8. What does Hebrews 13:6 say we can be bold about?

Every day we witness miracles that we know no human could perform. Evidence of God's presence and power is all around us in the universe. And yet we continue to search for peace outside of God, even when He is with us moment by moment on our journey.

Thelma Wells

9. Every verse of Scripture can give us some tidbit, some new facet of understanding.

- Who does Acts 5:32 say God gives the Holy Spirit to?

- According to Hebrews 6:4, what have we become?

DIGGING DEEPER

The Holy Spirit is our Helper. He comes to our aid whenever we need it. In the Psalms, David spoke often about the Lord's ability to come to the aid of those who looked to Him for it. It was a matter of both thanksgiving and praise in the Psalms.

- Psalm 22:19
- Psalm 70:5
- Psalm 35:2
- Psalm 86:5

Ponder & Pray

Have you ever thought you could use a little help? There's nothing easy about our daily lives or our spiritual walks. Many of us have complex responsibilities that weigh us down and unrealistic expectations that discourage us. When these moments come, we need to know that the Help we long for is closer than we think! What are some of the things you wish you could have help with? Are they things God's Helper can give His aid in? Ask the Lord to show you how He can help, and thank Him for the aid He gives.

Trinket to Treasure

It's probably a little insulting to relegate the Holy Spirit to the role of sidekick, but we'll go with it for the sake of analogy. Your trinket this week is a superhero mask, to remind you that the best heroes travel in duos. Without a sidekick, the superhero would lead a lonely life. But a constant companion becomes someone to trust, to understand, to listen, to care, and to share their secrets. The Holy Spirit is our own closest companion—a friend, a confidant, and a Helper.

✦ NOTES & PRAYER REQUESTS ✦

CHAPTER 4

COHABITATION

"DO YOU NOT KNOW THAT YOU ARE THE TEMPLE OF GOD AND THAT THE SPIRIT OF GOD DWELLS IN YOU?"

1 Corinthians 3:16 NKJV

I met my husband at college, and we were friends for five years before we got married. We were both part of a small group of comrades that did everything together. We sat together in chapel, attended the same classes, played pool and foosball, went on late-night doughnut runs, sang in choir concerts, studied in the student center, and generally had a lot of fun. As time went by, it seemed as if we'd been through everything together. We were best friends. We knew each other so well, or so we thought. It wasn't until after we were married that we *really* got to know each other. As honest as you can be with your friends, I think you have to live with someone before full dis-

CLEARING ✦ THE ✦ COBWEBS

How many different roommates have you had over the years?

closure happens! Only then do you become intimately aware of your spouse's idiosyncrasies, habits, and preferences.

We've already talked about knowing God and being known by Him. God is our Father, our Friend, and our ever present Helper. But have you ever considered the fact that He's also your "roommate"? Your heart and soul share space with His Spirit. He knows you intimately because He lives with you and in you.

1. When Jesus came as a child, He was given a very special name. What does Matthew 1:23 say He would be called?

So what is the soul? It is the deepest aspect of ourselves, the spiritual part that cries out for heaven, that is made to be a dwelling place for God. Nothing and no one else can answer that thirst. It is the size of eternity.

Sheila Walsh

2. What was Jesus' prayer for us in John 17:21?

3. It all sounds like a riddle. "I in you and He in Me." But it's as simple as a children's song—"Into my heart, into my heart, come into my heart, Lord Jesus." What does Paul say Jesus does in Ephesians 3:17?

4. Who dwells in us, according to Romans 8:9?

5. How are we described in 1 Corinthians 3:16?

6. Paul doesn't stop with this statement. What do we learn further about our "roommate" in 1 Corinthians 6:19?

When I went off to college, I was told I would share a dorm room with two other girls—Heather and Martha. I'd never shared a bedroom before, and I was nervous. One of my biggest concerns was closet space. Did I have too many clothes? I needn't have worried. Martha breezed into the dorm and promptly appropriated half the closet for her extensive wardrobe. I'd never seen so many clothes! Heather and I meekly split the second half of the closet between us.

We share our heart of hearts with the Lord of Lords. But how much room do we actually allow Him to use? Do we give Him His due, or do ask Him to downsize? Do we allow Him to reign, or relegate Him to the corner of a closet?

7. If the presence of God's own Spirit in our hearts really means that we are no longer our own, how does that change our everyday lives? Are we really giving up anything, or are we simply doing what we do with a new purpose in view?

8. Interestingly enough, we are not alone in our use as a temple. All believers share the same Spirit in the same way. What does Paul say the Spirit is working out in our lives corporately, according to Ephesians 2:22?

Sometimes we search so hard for the miraculous that we miss the obvious reality of God's ever-present nearness.

Patsy Clairmont

9. What is the proper working of this corporate temple compared to in Ephesians 4:16?

DIGGING DEEPER

Look at these two sets of verses—two from the Old Testament and two from New Testament. How does the idea of cohabitation change between the two?

- Psalm 90:1
- John 14:10
- Psalm 91:9
- John 14:17

PONDER & PRAY

God is with us. It's a promise we can cling to and a fact we can rely on. Take time this week to ponder just what it means to have God dwelling with you. Have you ever felt Him to be so close to you before? Thank God for His presence, and pray for a greater sensitivity to Him.

TRINKET TO TREASURE

If you are a Christian, then the Holy Spirit dwells in you—that's the fact of the matter. But how much room are you allowing Him to use? How much influence are you allowing Him to have? This week's trinket is a hanger, to remind you to share your "closet space" equitably. Don't let your clutter push the Lord off to the side. He's supposed to reign in our hearts, not be relegated to a tiny, dark corner.

> *The fact is, when we take charge of a situation without consulting the wisdom of God, we always make a mess of it. Relationships get convoluted, hearts get broken, unfair and unkind words are spoken, egos are crushed, waves of doubt trouble us, distrust creeps in, guilt takes up residence, and emotions go haywire. Thangs ain't purty.*
>
> Thelma Wells

✦ NOTES & PRAYER REQUESTS ✦

CHAPTER 5

THIRD PERSON

"IN THE NAME OF THE FATHER AND
OF THE SON AND OF THE HOLY SPIRIT."

Matthew 28:19 NKJV

When it comes to relationships, triangles are tricky. When you have three little girls playing together, one always seems to come away in tears, insisting she's being left out. When three little boys play together, two always seem to gang up on the other one in their war games. Odd numbers are hard to keep in balance.

Interestingly enough, God exists in a trinity. He certainly has no trouble keeping in balance. Father, Son, and Holy Spirit—three in one. But I think we often look at the First, Second, and Third Persons of the trinity as having varying degrees of importance in our lives. God the Father gets the most respect. We think of Him as having all the

CLEARING
✦ THE ✦
COBWEBS

Do you know someone who always works faithfully behind the scenes?

power and authority. We address our prayers to Him. Jesus, the Son, is everyone's favorite. We celebrate His birth, admire His life, and honor the memory of His death with tears of gratefulness. He calls us His friend, and His resurrection makes our future life in heaven possible. But what about this Third Person? Is He in third place because He's less important? What's His role?

1. Though the Trinity is not specifically named in the Bible, we can see the three persons of the Trinity mentioned. What familiar phrase do we find in Matthew 28:19?

2. Third Person hardly means third rate. Let's look at the Spirit's doings throughout Scripture. What do we find the Spirit doing in Genesis 1:2?

3. What was the Third Person of the Trinity responsible for in Luke 1:35 and Matthew 1:20?

4. How is the Holy Spirit depicted in Luke 3:22?

5. What Trinity is mentioned by the beloved disciple in 1 John 5:7?

The most wonderful truth behind dealing with distractions is that we don't need to organize and plan with our natural ability alone. The Holy Spirit, who gives us everything we need, can lengthen or shorten time depending on what He wants us to accomplish. If we yield ourselves to Him, He will order our steps according to His purposes.

Thelma Wells

*T*here are people in this world who quietly go about their business without ever receiving praise or acknowledgement for their good work. Church is a good place to take these folks for granted. They sweep up and lock doors. They manage the sound system. They wash blankets in the nursery. They fill paper towel dispensers. They change toner cartridges in copy machines. They water plants. These people do their jobs without ever calling attention to themselves. In fact, they are only made conspicuous by their absence. They keep things running so smoothly, it never occurs to us how those things get done! We take it for granted that the lawn will be mowed and the coffee will be hot and the toilet paper will be stocked.

Often the Holy Spirit is taken for granted because He works quietly behind the scenes in our lives. We don't realize just how much He does in our lives. Things just seem to get done. It doesn't always occur to us that Someone is doing all the work. Do *you* know what the Spirit's role in a believer's life is?

6. What else can we learn about the Holy Spirit from the Word? Each of these verses gives us a little insight. Match the description of the Spirit's work with the verse in which it can be found.

___ Acts 2:4	a. God is worshiped in the Spirit.
___ Romans 1:4	b. By the Spirit, the Gospel is preached.
___ Philippians 3:3	c. The Spirit moved men to prophesy.
___ Hebrews 10:15	d. The Spirit gave utterance for speaking in tongues.
___ 1 Peter 1:12	e. The Holy Spirit witnesses to us.
___ 2 Peter 1:21	f. Power is according to the Spirit.

7. What does 1 John 5:6 tell us that the Spirit is?

8. What does John 6:63 say that the Spirit does?

> *God pursues us, courts us, and woos us to remind us. His love changes every day; it either intensifies, or my understanding of it grows, but I don't think it really matters which it is.*
>
> Nicole Johnson

9. Why is the Spirit's presence in our hearts so vital to our spiritual lives, according to 1 Corinthians 2:11?

DIGGING DEEPER

It's hard to appreciate something you're not even aware of. How can you be thankful for the Spirit's working in your life if you don't even know what that work might be? For our Digging Deeper assignment this week, I'd like to encourage you to locate a Bible dictionary, Bible encyclopedia, or better yet a topical Bible, and look up "Holy Spirit." As you read through these articles, make a list for yourself of the role of the Holy Spirit in your life.

PONDER & PRAY

This week, make it your prayer to take nothing for granted. Ask for an awareness of the Spirit's working in your heart and life. Keep your eyes and ears open for signs of His hand. Ask the Spirit to help you as you pray—it's one of the things He does best!

TRINKET TO TREASURE

The image we most often associate with the third person of the trinity is the dove, so we'll make that our trinket for this week. Whenever you look at your little winged messenger, it can remind you that though the Spirit holds a place of essential importance in every believer's life. Let's not take Him for granted.

CHAPTER 6

SEALED

"HAVING BELIEVED, YOU WERE SEALED WITH THE HOLY SPIRIT OF PROMISE."

Ephesians 1:13 NKJV

My sister is the funny one in the family. She can tell stories that leave people weak in the knees, with tears running down their cheeks. When we were growing up together, she used to do the funniest thing. We'd come into the kitchen, where Mom was cooking, and there'd be something good spread out on the table. My sister would look over the array of food, make sure she had everyone's attention, then slowly and deliberately lick her finger. Before anyone could stop her, she'd plant her finger on the middle of a slice of pizza or a cupcake or something and announce, "That one's mine!" Nobody ever argued with her.

CLEARING ✦ THE ✦ COBWEBS

Did you ever have something you loved so much that you carved your name onto it (literally or figuratively)?

Whenever I read a verse that talks about God using His Holy Spirit to seal believers for Himself, I have a picture in my mind of Him licking His finger and placing it on my forehead and announcing, "That one's Mine!" Where God places His seal, no one can argue His ownership.

1. Our salvation is a singularly personal and intimate transformation. Jesus compares it with being born again—born of the Spirit.

John 3:5 – "Most assuredly, I say to you, unless one is _____ of _____ and the _____, he cannot _____ the _____ of God" (NKJV).

John 3:6 – "That which is _____ of the _____ is _____, and that which is _____ of the _____ is _____" (NKJV).

2. What does Paul say that the Spirit has done in our hearts, according to 1 Corinthians 6:11?

> We all have a specific task to do for God, and it was planned in His head before we were ever formed in the womb. That is an incredible truth.
>
> Marilyn Meberg

3. Paul is very specific about the Spirit's role in our hearts. Why does he say God gave us His Spirit in 2 Corinthians 1:22 and again in 2 Corinthians 5:5?

4. When does Paul say we were sealed by the Spirit, according to Ephesians 1:13?

5. In these verses, the Spirit seems to be compared to a deposit, a down payment, or earnest money. He's our guarantee that we'll come into a great deal more one day. What are we sealed for, according to Ephesians 4:30?

I know a guy who likes to go to flea markets. He meanders through tables laden with one man's trash and another man's treasures. But he doesn't wander aimlessly. He's got a sharp eye for a good buy, because he's educated himself to know what things are worth. What one person finds useless and worthless might be priceless to an avid collector. Sifting through all the replicas and reproductions is a cinch if you know the marks of the genuine article. These marks authenticate a piece and raise its value from trash to treasure.

The Spirit is God's mark on our lives. You could say His presence in our hearts authenticates our salvation. He is God's unmistakable stamp of ownership. He testifies to our genuineness. He is our Maker's mark, and He elevates us from trash to treasure.

6. Paul gets even more specific about what we've been sealed for in Ephesians 1:14. What does he say the Spirit is in this verse?

7. The Spirit seals us and serves as a guarantee against our future inheritance, but that's not all He does. In the whole salvation process, the Spirit's role is vital in so many unseen ways! Take a look at what He does, and match each action with the appropriate verse.

___ Romans 15:16   a. He justifies us.

___ 2 Thessalonians 2:13   b. He makes us acceptable to God.

___ 1 Timothy 3:16   c. He makes us alive.

___ Titus 3:5   d. He sanctifies us when we believe.

___ 1 Peter 3:18   e. He washes, renews, and regenerates us.

8. The Spirit's seal on our lives is a vital part of our salvation, and yet we often take Him and His work for granted. David was one man who was keenly aware of the Spirit's place in his heart. What was David's earnest prayer in Psalm 51:11?

> *When we give ourselves to God—mind, body, soul, and spirit—He changes us. We cannot change ourselves. We don't have enough spiritual stamina to change ourselves, let alone another person or the world. But when the walls come down and He has access to the deepest parts of who we are, His love courses through us in a cleansing, holy way.*
>
> Nicole Johnson

9. There is much encouragement in this week's lesson. God wants us
He knows us. And He's claimed us for His own. We bear His mark, hav
ing been sealed by His Spirit as a guarantee for the future He's promise
to us. What promise can we cling to, as it i
found in 2 Timothy 2:19?

> *The Creator has made us
> each one of a kind. There
> is nobody else exactly like
> us, and there never will be.
> Each of us is his special
> creation and is alive for a
> distinctive purpose.
> Because of this, the person
> we are, and the
> contribution we make by
> being that very person, are
> vitally important to God.*
>
> Luci Swindoll

DIGGING DEEPER

It doesn't take much digging to turn up the fact that God
lays claim to whatever He wants. Throughout Scripture,
He tells us "Everything under heaven is Mine" (Job 41:11
NKJV). For a little extra exploration, look at these verses in
which God says, "This is Mine."

- Exodus 19:5
- Ezekiel 18:4
- Psalm 50:11–12
- Haggai 2:8

PONDER & PRAY

What a wonderful thing to be confident of: God loves us, knows us, and claims us as His own. He brought you into His family and put His seal upon your soul. He exclaims, "Mine! This one's Mine!" This week, marvel over the fact of your belonging to God. May it inspire many a prayer of praise in the week to come.

TRINKET TO TREASURE

When I was taught the song "Puff the Magic Dragon" in kindergarten, I wondered what "ceiling wax" might be. It puzzled me to no end until, much later, I learned that in the days before lick and stick envelopes *sealing* wax was used to secure papers for post. This week's trinket is sealing wax, to remind us that we have been sealed by God. We bear Him image. We've been claimed as His own. And we are sealed for eternity by His Spirit.

✦ NOTES & PRAYER REQUESTS ✦

CHAPTER 7

UNDENIABLE POWER

"IN DEMONSTRATION OF THE SPIRIT AND OF POWER."

1 Corinthians 2:4 NKJV

Is there an "amen" section in your congregation? Does your sanctuary have stained glass windows and candles? During worship, do your brothers and sisters dance up and down the aisles? Do responsive readings figure into your service? Is there a pipe organ for accompanying the singing of hymns? During the praise songs, is the air filled with hands raised in worship? Do your youth take turns at the electric guitars and drums?

There's no doubt that God has a place for all kinds of folks in His Church. I've always said that variety is the spice of life, and I find the astonishing diversity among believers to be fascinating. Believers throughout the world run the range from hushed liturgy to

CLEARING
✦ THE ✦
COBWEBS

When's the most memorable time you were inconvenienced because a battery died and you lost power for something?

charismatic exuberance. Each of us glorifies God in our own way, no matter where we fall in that range. But no matter how we choose to express ourselves, no one can deny the real power of God's Spirit in our midst.

1. What was Jesus' parting message to His disciples according to Acts 1:8?

2. The word for Spirit in Scripture could literally be translated "wind." That makes some sense considering the entrance the Holy Spirit makes in Acts 2:2–4. How is His coming described?

The realization that God intends for each of us greater power than we are currently experiencing is tremendously encouraging.

Marilyn Meberg

3. In Acts 10:38, what does Peter say that God anointed Jesus with?

4. The presence of the Holy Spirit often comes in tandem with power from on high. But power isn't the only thing that goes hand in hand with Him. Or maybe we should say that with the Holy Spirit's presence comes the power to do...what?

 • How was the power of the Spirit demonstrated in Paul's life, according to 1 Corinthians 2:4?

 • How does 1 Thessalonians 1:5 say that the gospel was able to reach the churches?

• We find the same idea in the Old Testament. What did the prophet declare the Spirit gave him power to do, according to Micah 3:8?

5. As powerful as God's message is and has been through the ages, we cannot limit the Spirit's power to the words He gives to us. The Spirit's power is not in word only, but also in deed! What did Isaiah 61:1 say that the Spirit would give Messiah the power to do?

*I*t's so simple. It's so basic. Every time I do it, I have to shake my head and laugh. Do you ever forget to plug things in too? I'm always puzzled at first, jiggling switches and poking at buttons. "Who broke this?" Vacuum cleaners, toasters, popcorn poppers, computers, lamps, answering machines, cassette players, televisions. I even forgot to re-plug in our big freezer in the garage once. On one memorable Sunday, we arrived home from church to find a cold crock-pot with a raw chicken sitting on the kitchen counter. I'd turned the crock-pot on but hadn't plugged it in. Electrical appliances simply don't work if you don't allow electricity to flow into them!

We don't work so well without power either. A Christian isn't meant to function on her own wherewithal. We need the Spirit's power if we're going to get anything done!

6. The Spirit has power to do amazing things. What happened through the Spirit's power in Acts 8:39?

7. What does Romans 15:19 say was accomplished by the power of the Spirit of God?

When I need power for anything (my wild boar meat strainer or vegetable puree–mash mixer) I plug in. Simple. So am I not "plugged in" to God's power? After all, I am a Christian...I study my Bible...I pray. What am I missing?

Marilyn Meberg

8. What important principle do we often need to be reminded of, as it is found in Zechariah 4:6?

9. What reminder, encouragement, and promise do we find in 2 Timothy 1:7?

DIGGING DEEPER

The Holy Spirit equips us with the power we need to do the things we need to do. What else is invaluable for equipping the believer, according to 2 Timothy 3:14–17?

PONDER & PRAY

The gift of the Holy Spirit doesn't come with the asterisk and small print revealing "Batteries Not Included." He comes fully equipped to equip us for living. This week, consider the power that God has made available to you. Thank God for His gift and ask Him to show you how to tap into it.

TRINKET TO TREASURE

This week we need a reminder that with the Holy Spirit, we receive the power we need for spiritual living. He's our Source and resource. He equips us for the tasks God places before us. We only run into trouble when we *don't* tap in. So this week's little treasure is one of those little child-proof outlet covers. When they're in place, they block the flow of power because we can't plug in. Leave this little reminder *un*plugged so that you can tap in to the Spirit's flow.

God never calls without enabling us. In other words, if he calls you to do something, he makes it possible for you to do it.

Luci Swindoll

✦ NOTES & PRAYER REQUESTS ✦

CHAPTER 8

QUIET INFLUENCE

"PRAYING ALWAYS WITH ALL PRAYER AND SUPPLICATION IN THE SPIRIT."

Ephesians 6:18 NKJV

My dad always plants a big vegetable garden. Every summer we'd spend an hour or so in the evenings weeding and watering. The spigot for the garden hose was located in the old cement foundation of a barn—open to the sky and overhung with trees. Though it is completely surrounded by stone and cement, the area just surrounding that spigot is green with a lush carpet of moss. Why? Because the tap leaks. It isn't much, but the steady dripping of water is enough to sustain this tiny spot of greenery. A little at a time, slow and steady, quietly dripping, is sufficient to bring about this transformation.

CLEARING ✦ THE ✦ COBWEBS

When you get out into the summer sun, do you tan, burn, freckle, or peel?

The Holy Spirit works that way in our hearts. Quiet and unseen, slow and constant. He works in the very foundations of our hearts, bringing about a transformation. The Spirit's influence in our lives isn't always easy to see, but it's always present.

1. What rhetorical question does Isaiah pose in Isaiah 40:13?

2. We should never presume to direct God's hand for Him. Indeed, the New Testament is filled with illustrations of believers who've learned the wisdom of letting the Spirit do the directing!

• How did Jesus decide what to do in Luke 4:1?

• According to Philippians 1:19, what was Paul confident about and why?

3. We even find instances in Scripture when the Spirit wasn't quite so quiet! What did the Spirit say and do in Acts 13:2, 4?

4. The Spirit's influence may be quiet, but the results of His influence are often astonishing and very visible. What did Jesus tell us we could depend upon the Spirit for in Mark 13:11 and in Luke 12:12?

5. Words have always been the Spirit's "thing." What does 2 Samuel 23:2 say about the Spirit of the Lord?

*I*n the summer as the temperatures rise, we dress in lighter clothes. Sweaters and jeans are replaced by sleeveless shirts and khaki shorts. And in the first weeks of summer, something inevitable happens. I get my first sunburn of the year. A day at the zoo or a picnic in the park is all it takes. Unnoticed, unheeded, and unrelenting, the sun singes. Afterwards, it's easy to see the solar influence on my shoulders, the back of my neck, on across my nose.

The Spirit's quiet influence is often just that way. Unnoticed and unheeded at the time, but clearly seen in hindsight.

6. Don't you wish the Spirit would exercise Himself in some miraculous way now and then in your life? Quieter influences are so hard to trace. Knowing the right thing to say at the right time may not seem like much, but it's such a practical gift. There are other practical ways the Spirit works in our midst.

• What is the Holy Spirit credited with doing in Acts 9:31?

• What does the Spirit use its influence to foster, according to Philippians 2:1?

7. There's another way the Holy Spirit uses His quiet influence in our lives. It's mentioned in these three verses. Can you find the common thread?

Jude 1:20 – "You, beloved, _____ yourselves up on your most holy _____, _____ in the _____ _____" (NKJV).

1 Corinthians 14:15 – "I will _____ with the _____, and I will also _____ with the _____. I will _____ with the _____, and I will also _____ with the _____" (NKJV).

Ephesians 6:18 – "_____ always with all _____ and _____ in the _____" (NKJV).

8. Sometimes the Spirit's way with words is just what we need. How does Romans 8:26 say that He helps us?

> *How does one find God? He is in our prayers guiding our words, He is in our songs as we worship Him, and He is filling our mouths when we comfort a friend or speak wisdom to someone who needs hope.*
>
> Patsy Clairmont

9. The Spirit *is* a quiet influencer in our lives—no fireworks, parades, or even rushing winds. We don't always see what He's up to in our lives. But we can learn to listen for His quiet nudging. What lesson did Elijah learn in 1 Kings 19:12?

DIGGING DEEPER

When the Spirit of the Lord is at work, most often words are involved. Throughout Scriptures we see the two go hand in hand—the Spirit of the Lord comes over someone and they speak.

- Matthew 10:20
- Mark 12:36
- Ephesians 6:17

PONDER & PRAY

We often remember that the Lord comes to us with a still, small voice, but we find it hard to remember to listen for that quiet prompting. The Spirit's influence in our lives is largely a quiet one, and it will go completely unnoticed if we aren't sensitive to His ways. This week, pray for a heightened sensitivity to His quiet influence in your heart. Perhaps He'll help you put your discoveries into words.

TRINKET TO TREASURE

Since the quiet and constant influence of the Spirit can be illustrated by the unmistakable influence of the sun on our unprotected skin, we'll choose sunscreen as our trinket this week. We may not see the Spirit's hand in our lives until the evidence becomes clear later on, but that doesn't mean He's not by our sides all along the way.

> *The Lord called us to be a peculiar people. Not strange in the sense we act bizarre, but peculiar in the ways we respond to life because the Lord's Spirit is working within us.*
>
> Patsy Clairmont

✦ Notes & Prayer Requests ✦

CHAPTER 9

Housewarming Gifts

"Now concerning spiritual gifts, brethren,
I do not want you to be ignorant."

1 Corinthians 12:1 NKJV

The giving of housewarming gifts is an old tradition. They're a way to help friends and neighbors settle in and celebrate their new home. Lots of things make nice housewarming gifts. We've given everything from birdfeeders and apple trees to quilts and apple pies. These gifts can be beautiful or practical or even silly. Someone I know always gives a set of pink flamingoes to new homeowners. One year, our church did a "pounding" for a family. This is a tradition that dates back to the days of the American frontier. Neighbors would welcome a new family into the area by holding

Clearing
✦ the ✦
Cobwebs

Do you still keep up the tradition of bringing a hostess gift to a party?

a pounding. Each family would bring a pound of something as a gift. A pound of butter, flour, sugar, bacon, or beans might be added to the newcomers' pantry. A pound of nails could be put right to work during a barn-raising. In modern-day poundings, folks generally just bring non-perishable food items.

When we were saved and the Holy Spirit took up residence in our hearts, He didn't come empty-handed. His housewarming gifts equip us for our lives as believers. They're always beautiful, and eminently practical.

1. What did Jesus accomplish on our behalf when He ascended into heaven after His resurrection?

2. When did Peter say people would receive the gift of the Holy Spirit, according to Acts 2:38?

3. A gift! Salvation was a gift. Now we discover that the Spirit is a gift—and one that keeps on giving! What does Matthew 7:11 tell us about God's gifts?

> *Jesus longs for us to experience radical transformation of what comes naturally. Isn't that outlandish? All I can say is it's a good thing our God is big because, if we're going to be that different from our human nature, He's going to be very busy.*
>
> Patsy Clairmont

4. James tells of God's gifts as well. What does he declare in James 1:17?

5. What does Paul tell us about the gifts God gives us in Romans 11:29?

*H*ave you ever taken a spiritual gifts inventory? It's a tool used by Christians to help understand the ways God has uniquely gifted us. Taking the test brings back memories of standardized tests in grade school, with two sharpened number two pencils close at hand. But at the end of the process, patterns take shape. Your strengths and preferences and likes and interests reveal God's hand in gifting you for your place in His Church. Such a tool can be very helpful, for you can't always use a gift if you don't even know you have it! And once you find you've got them, you can find ways of using them in your own church home. Our spiritual gifts help us to find our niche!

6. What does 1 Corinthians 12:4 remind us about our spiritual gifts?

7. What does Paul, who clearly had the gift of exhortation, tell us to do with our spiritual gifts in Romans 12:6?

8. What should our attitude be toward spiritual gifts, according to 1 Corinthians 12:31 and 1 Corinthians 14:1?

9. Why did Paul say we should be zealous for spiritual gifts in 1 Corinthians 14:12?

> *It is easy to believe that God can use our lives when we see immediate results, when positive feedback encourages us to push on. It is hard to keep walking when we see little sign that what we are doing is making a difference.*
>
> Sheila Walsh

DIGGING DEEPER

What are some of the spiritual gifts mentioned in Scripture?

- Acts 2:4
- 1 Corinthians 12:8, 9
- 1 Corinthians 12:28, 30

PONDER & PRAY

Have you ever wondered if your personality, tastes, likes, and passions are indicators of the spiritual gifts you've been given? Ponder the various spiritual gifts in the coming week and ask the Lord to show you which ones are strongly present in your hearts. Ask Him to show you how He would like you to put those gifts to work in your life. He may just surprise you!

TRINKET TO TREASURE

A gift is a gift is a gift, but a gift that's been tied with a ribbon is simply sublime. Your trinket for remembering God's spiritual gifts simply has to be ribbon—striped, dotted, zigzagged, or zany—any design that suits your fancy.

Whiners neither enjoy nor give joy. But grace-filled people are reputable, sought after, and deeply loved.

Patsy Clairmont

CHAPTER 10

FRUIT

But the fruit of the Spirit is love,
joy, peace, longsuffering, kindness,
goodness, faithfulness, gentleness, self-
control. Against such there is no law."

Galatians 5:22–23 NKJV

've always rather liked the brand name Fruit of the Loom™. Though the label for these wardrobe "foundations" depicts actual fruit, the company is not implying that Dad's boxers and briefs came from textile orchards. The name simply implies that the t-shirts and undies we buy at K-Mart are the end result of the weaver's work on their looms. We're talking fruit as in "the fruit of our labors" here.

Fruit speaks of outcomes, consequences, and the culmination of our hard work. *Fruit* is the finished product. It's the tangible evidence of one's efforts. It's the end result. It's the reward we reap and the harvest we've labored for. Scripture talks about spiritual fruit. It too is the visible

CLEARING ✦ THE ✦ COBWEBS

What is one tangible thing that you can identify as a "fruit of your labor"?

evidence of work—the Spirit's working in our hearts. As we experience the intimacy of the Holy Spirit's presence, our lives confirm His good influence. These unmistakable signs are the fruit He nurtures—the fruit of the Spirit.

1. Jesus used gardening to illustrate spiritual principles. His comments are so straightforward, they seem to ring with good, old common sense.

Matthew 7:17–18 – "Even so, every _____ tree _____ _____ fruit, but a _____ tree _____ _____ fruit. A _____ tree cannot _____ _____ fruit, nor can a _____ _____ bear _____ fruit" (NKJV).

Matthew 12:33 – "Either make the _____ _____ and its _____ _____, or else make the _____ _____ and its _____ _____; for a _____ is _____ by its _____" (NKJV).

Luke 6:44 – "For every _____ is _____ by its own _____. For men do not gather _____ from _____, nor do they gather _____ from a _____ _____" (NKJV).

2. The condition of the heart can affect the fruit it brings forth. What does Jesus say interferes with the fruitfulness of our lives in Luke 8:14?

3. In Luke 8:15, what heart characteristics are conducive to fruitfulness?

> *God wastes nothing. Not our joys, not our sorrows—nothing.*
>
> Nicole Johnson

4. Paul says, "He who sows sparingly will also reap sparingly, and he who sows bountifully will also reap bountifully" (2 Cor. 9:6 NKJV). What should we be sowing in ourselves, according to Hosea 10:12?

5. One thing we must never forget: We depend on the Lord for any spiritual growth and fruit we might see.

- According to John 15:2, what does the Lord do to encourage fruit production?

• According to Hebrews 12:11, what training is necessary to yield good and righteous fruit in our lives?

• What is absolutely necessary if we want to live fruitful lives, according to John 15:4?

• What contrast does John 15:5 set up between those who abide in Jesus and those who do not?

There's an old saying that says, "The apple doesn't fall far from the tree." Generally this means that children are very much like their parents—temperaments, traits, talents, and tendencies are often passed on to the next generation. Family resemblances come in many ways. For instance, my mom, my sister and I all have the same voice. We're nearly indistinguishable over the telephone. (If we could sing, we'd probably make a great trio!)

As Christians, we belong to a family—God's own. Have you ever given any thought as to the family resemblance that believers bear? How are we like our Father? How are we like our brothers and sisters?

6. According to John 15:16, what have we as Jesus' disciples been appointed to do?

7. Why should we strive to live fruitful lives according to John 15:8?

> *You might appear to be different—or even strange—to some people. But remember, God made you in His image for His glory. Use your uniqueness to edify people and glorify God. Capitalize on the abilities God has given you.*
>
> Thelma Wells

8. In order to bear spiritual fruit, Scripture says we must trust the Spirit to grow us up into maturity. What do each of these verses urge us to do?

• Galatians 5:16 – "_____ in the Spirit" (NKJV).

• Galatians 5:18 – "_____by the Spirit" (NKJV).

• Galatians 5:25 – "_____ in the Spirit" (NKJV).

9. So, the fruit of the Spirit is the result of God's work in our hearts through His Spirit. It's the evidence of His presence and the overflow of His influence in our lives. Just what does this fruit look like, according to these verses?

• Galatians 5:22–23

• Ephesians 5:9

DIGGING DEEPER

The Bible's lesson is simple—you reap what you sow. When applied to good things, it's all good. But there are two sides to this principle, and we cannot ignore the less appealing truth. How does Paul address this matter in Galatians 6:7–9? What encouragement does he leave with us in verse nine?

PONDER & PRAY

Have you ever wondered how your life might be bearing fruit and giving glory to God? This week's lesson gives us a good idea of what our lives should look like if the Spirit is having His influence in our lives. In the days ahead, ponder the possibilities of your fruitfulness. Ask the Lord to do His good pruning and training so that you can bear fruit for His glory.

TRINKET TO TREASURE

We all want to live fruitful lives which bring glory to God. Since this week's lesson has focused on fruit, our trinket this week will be the beginning of all fruitfulness—seeds. The Spirit has been implanted into our hearts, and the potential is there for a full and ripe harvest. When you look at your packet of seeds, pray that the Spirit's work in your heart will bring forth the good fruit God desires.

✦ Notes & Prayer Requests ✦

CHAPTER 11

FILL 'ER UP!

"AND THE DISCIPLES WERE FILLED
WITH JOY AND WITH THE HOLY SPIRIT."

Acts 13:52 NKJV

A trip to the gas station for our family can be quite an event. The kids can't wait for the gauge to dip down below a quarter of a tank, because they look forward to the refueling ritual. Daddy pumps the gas while Mama herds the troops in for potty breaks. Then everyone mans the squeegees, washing windows, mirrors, headlights, taillights, and license plates. The garbage can is emptied. Tire pressure is checked. The hood is popped, and the fluids are checked. Mileage is noted. Travel odometer reset to zero. Then we pull around back for the brushless carwash.

While our car is getting its beauty treatment, I like to watch others at the pumps. They act like a NASCAR pit crew, trying

CLEARING
✦ THE ✦
COBWEBS

Have you ever run out of gasoline and had to make the long, slow walk to a gas station for a gallon of fuel?

to get in and out as quickly as possible. They're fueling on the fly, not willing to take the time involved in filling the tank all the way to the top. They'll pull over just long enough to put a few dollars worth of gasoline into their tank. Just enough to keep moving. No time for more. Too busy to linger.

This tendency to rush often carries over into our spiritual lives. We run ourselves down until we're running on empty. Then, when its time to refuel, we skimp. It takes time to really fill up the tank, but we're too busy to linger. So we dribble a little into the tank and rush off.

1. There's some difference between the fact that we are indwelt by the Holy Spirit and the filling of the Holy Spirit. The spirit lives in our hearts because we have been saved. He's always with us and seals us for all eternity. But just because we have Him doesn't mean we're *filled* by Him.

- What did the prophet say God would do in Isaiah 44:3?

- What does Acts 2:33 tell us Jesus did when He returned to His Father's side?

- What prophecy, found in Joel 2:28–29, was fulfilled in Acts 2:17–18?

2. When it came to the Spirit, God expressed His plan for giving in terms of pouring. God was fond of pouring out blessings on His people. How does Malachi 3:10 describe this generous method of distribution?

3. The Father is abundant with His gifts, and that includes the gift of the Spirit. God wants to fill us to overflowing with His Spirit, but He cannot do it if we are full of ourselves.

Psalm 23:5 – "My cup _____ _____" (NKJV).

John 3:34 – "God does not _____ the _____ by _____" (NKJV).

John 10:10 – "I have come that they may have _____, and that they may have it _____ _____" (NKJV).

2 Corinthians 9:8 – "God is able to make _____ grace _____ toward you, that you, _____ having _____ _____ in _____ things, may have an _____ for every good work" (NKJV).

Ephesians 3:20 – "Now to Him who is able to do _____ _____ _____ all that we _____ or _____, according to the power that works in us" (NKJV).

Titus 3:6 – "Whom He _____ _____ on us _____ through Jesus Christ our Savior" (NKJV).

4. So how does this filling come about? All in a rush? Only after long meditation? Automatically? After we pray for it? When we are at our weakest? When we show great inner strength? What does Ephesians 5:18 contrast the filling of the Spirit with?

5. What we are filled with influences our attitudes and our actions. We are invited to be filled with the Spirit. What else does Paul urge us to be filled with?

• Philippians 1:11

• Colossians 1:9

*Y*ou've probably seen it sometime, in a comedy routine. The consummate waiter offers to fill a customer's cup for them—"Say when." But the customer is distracted by something else going on in the restaurant, and fails to give the signal to cease. So the waiter continues to pour, even after the cup overflows into the saucer and dribbles over onto the tablecloth.

When the Lord says He wants to fill us with His spirit, He's not stingy about it. He doesn't just offer to fill us to the brim. He wants to fill us until we're brimming over.

6. The psalmist declares, "My heart is overflowing with a good theme" (Ps. 45:1 NKJV). What are the ways in which we can be filled? There are so many, let's do a quick overview. In each of these verses, what are we filled with?

- **Psalm 107:9** – God fills the hungry soul with _____

- **Psalm 126:2** – Our mouths are filled with _____

- **Habakkuk 2:14** – The earth will be filled with _____

- **Matthew 5:6** – Those who hunger and thirst for it will be filled with
_____

- **John 15:11** – Jesus assures us that we can be filled with
_____

- **Acts 14:17** – God fills our hearts with _____

- **Romans 15:13** – The God of hope fills us with _____

- **Romans 15:14** – We are full of _____

- **James 3:17** – The wisdom we gain from God is full of

    _____

7. In our opening illustration, we talked about rushing around and never taking the time to fill up when we're running dry. So how do we make the conscious shift from hurry, hurry, hurry to hearing the Spirit's call and bending to His instruction? Scripture encourages us to stop and consider.

- What does God tell Job to do in Job 37:14?

- In Psalm 8:3–4, what stirs David's thoughts into meditation?

- What does Paul urge his young protégé to consider in 2 Timothy 2:7?

8. There are many ways to say it—consider, ponder, meditate. It means slowing down, tuning in, noticing, listening. It doesn't have to be a time-consuming process, but it does have to happen.

• According to Psalm 143:5, what should we meditate on?

• What should fill our mind at the close of each day, according to Psalm 77:6?

• As we look ahead, what should the focus of our meditation be, according to Psalm 119:15?

In our relationship with God, we can run through our days ignoring our need for Him—intentionally or unintentionally—until we find ourselves dry and worn out.

Sheila Walsh

9. We cannot consider anything that isn't already in our minds. Meditation happens when we have something to mull over. What should we fill our heads with according to Joshua 1:8?

DIGGING DEEPER

Those who were filled with the Spirit were enabled to do amazing things. Through His divine influence, the Lord empowered them to do just what needed to be done. Take a look at these two examples.

- Exodus 31:3
- 1 Kings 7:14

PONDER & PRAY

Just as a sponge can be filled with water—every hole, pore, niche, and nook—we can be saturated by the Spirit. Just as a person who is drunk acts under the influence of the spirits he consumed, we can be filled with the Spirit and live under His influence. Ask the Lord for this kind of filling. He's ready to pour through you.

TRINKET TO TREASURE

Our spiritual life cannot flourish without the Spirit pouring through our lives. We need His filling, His permeation, His saturation. Our lives can brim over with the Spirit's influence. To remind us of this, our trinket for the week is a pitcher. When we're being filled by the Spirit, the supply never ends.

> *Even though I know I need that intimate communication that settles my soul, I still run on blindly at times, not willing to stop and get the refreshment that would revitalize my whole being.*
>
> Sheila Walsh

✦ NOTES & PRAYER REQUESTS ✦

CHAPTER 12

SPIRITUAL INTIMACY

"EVERYONE WHO CONFESSES THAT JESUS IS
GOD'S SON PARTICIPATES CONTINUOUSLY
IN AN INTIMATE RELATIONSHIP WITH GOD."

1 John 4:15 MSG

I just had a watercolor painting lesson from my mother. Frankly, I found it a little unnerving. My comfort zone is a well-ordered place. I like logical, systematic, point A to point B processes. First you do this. Then you do that. In the end, you will have this. Simple. Comprehensive. Tidy. But Mom thought it was time I learned to loosen up a little, so she gave me a lesson in abstractions. "There's no wrong way to do this. Just let the colors flow together. You never know what you're going to get." Ack! For a girl who doesn't like to let her food touch on her plate, letting the green splotch run into the purple splotch threw me into uncertain territory.

CLEARING ✦ THE ✦ COBWEBS

Do you like to learn as you go, experimenting in a trial-and-error method, or do you prefer to do things by the book, following step-by-step instructions?

Wouldn't it be nice if our Bibles were arranged with simple, comprehensive instructions to spiritual intimacy? A nice, all-encompassing manual to better prayer and praise. A step-by-step process for efficient quiet times. A checklist for bringing glory to God in daily life. Tips. Techniques. Systems. Strategies. But it just isn't so. Each of us moves forward as a unique individual, building a relationship with the Spirit in our own way. There's no wrong way to do it. Our life and His just kind of flow together, and we never really know what it'll become. All we can do is hang on to the promise that it'll be something beautiful.

1. What can you be sure of in your walk in the Spirit? What do you have to take by faith?

2. "Intimate" is not a word we run across much in Scripture translations. So when we want to gain a sense of what spiritual intimacy with the Holy Spirit is, it helps to turn to the modern paraphrases. What does Peter say is ours through our intimate relationship with Christ?

> *Everything that goes into a life of pleasing God has been miraculously given to us by getting to know, personally and intimately, the One who invited us to God. The best invitation we ever received!*
> —2 Peter 1:3 MSG

3. Intimacy requires interaction and interdependence. How does John 15:5 describe our intimate relationship with the Lord in this modern paraphrase?

> *I am the Vine, you are the branches. When you're joined with me and I with you, the relation intimate and organic, the harvest is sure to be abundant.* —John 15:5 MSG

4. Have you ever thought of your life with the Lord as a living thing—capable of change and growth? What areas of growth would you like to see in your own life, with the Spirit's help?

If I could say only one thing, it would be simple and to the point: God knows all about you. He knows your good days and your bad days. He knows the noble thoughts and the shameful thoughts. He sees your devotion and your indifference. And he loves you—totally, completely, passionately, boundlessly. Forever.

Sheila Walsh

5. What should we never take for granted, according to this version o
Ephesians 4:30?

> *His Holy Spirit, moving and breathing in you, is the most inti-mate part of your life, making you fit for himself. Don't take such a gift for granted.* —Ephesians 4:30 MSG

We mostly hear about intimacy as it relates to mar-ried couples, but it's certainly not limited to this. Generally speaking, intimacy speaks of close association and famil-iarity. Intimacy involves one's deepest feelings and the vul-nerability of sharing those feelings with a trusted friend. An intimate is a close friend or confidant. They're the ones we trust with our very personal and very private thoughts. The trust required in this kind of friendship can take years to build.

In some ways, the hardest part of intimacy has already been surmounted when it comes to the Lord. He already knows our innermost thoughts and feelings. We take no risks in entrusting ourselves to Him. The Spirit is a confi-dant we can trust and love.

6. What does Paul pray for us in Ephesians 3:16?

7. What is happening in our lives by the Spirit, according to 2 Corinthians 3:18?

8. What three things belong to us, according to 2 Corinthians 13:14?

> *We are loved passionately by God. And I don't know why. It is a mystery, and it must remain a mystery...I don't have a clue why God loves me. But I believe in the core of my being that He does. So I surrender to it. I stop fighting it. I cease trying to figure it out. I collapse on it.*
>
> Nicole Johnson

9. Let's take our benediction for this study from Paul in Romans 15:13. What does he ask for us from the Lord?

DIGGING DEEPER

The last twelve chapters have focused on our relationship with God, especially with His third person—the Holy Spirit. All of us want to deepen the intimacy we have in our spiritual lives. But to dig a little deeper, look at this verse from Paul. How does this verse challenge us further?

Don't hoard the experience for yourself. Pray for the insight and ability to bring others into that intimacy. –1 Corinthians 14:13 MSG

PONDER & PRAY

There's no checklist for achieving spiritual intimacy. As you move forward, it must be hand in hand with the Lord's Spirit. He'll teach you, guide you, influence you, and help you to deepen your love and trust in Him. He's your source of power, the carrier of prayers, the promise of eternity, and the quiet influencer. He is your Helper, the Comforter, the bearer of gifts and bringer of fruit. Praise God for His Spirit and for the relationship that can grow because of Him.

TRINKET TO TREASURE

As we pursue spiritual intimacy, we need to remember that there's no wrong way to go about it. Each of us has a relationship with the Lord as unique as we are. Our reminder of this will be a paintbrush. Just as a watercolorist is often surprised by the movement of water and paint across paper, we can be surprised by the Spirit's work in our hearts. Our life and His just kind of flow together, and we never really know what it'll become. All we can do is hang on to the promise that it'll be something beautiful.

SHALL WE REVIEW?

Every chapter has added a new trinket to your treasure trove of memories. Let's remind ourselves of the lessons they hold for us!

1. A walking stick.

This trinket provided something to lean on as we travel the well-worn trails of God's continued goodness. A steadying handhold as we explore new paths with awe-inspiring vistas. A familiar accompaniment as we revisit the landmarks of our spiritual walk.

2. A pennant.

Just as a fan yearns to know everything there is to know about the object of their affections, we are compelled to know God more and more. But while the average fan is just a face in the crowd and a stranger, we are recognized, known, and loved by our Lord.

3. A superhero mask.

The best heroes travel in duos. Without a sidekick, the super-hero would lead a lonely life. But a constant companion becomes someone to trust, to understand, to listen, to care, and to share secrets with. The Holy Spirit is our own closest companion—a friend, a confidant, and a Helper.

4. A hanger.

If you are a Christian, then the Holy Spirit dwells in you—that's the fact of the matter. But how much room are you allowing Him to use? How much influence are you allowing Him to have? This week's trinket is to remind you to share your "closet space" equitably.

5. A dove.

The image we most often associate with the third person of the trinity is the dove. Whenever you look at your little winged messenger, it can remind you that the Spirit holds a place of essential importance in every believer's life. Let's not take Him for granted.

6. Sealing wax.

This week's trinket reminds us that we have been sealed by God. We bear Him image. We've been claimed as His own. And we are sealed for eternity by His Spirit.

7. An outlet cover.

The Holy Spirit is our Source and resource. We only run into trouble when we *don't* tap in. When they're in place, outlet covers block the flow of power because we can't plug in. Leave this little reminder *un*plugged so that you can tap in to the Spirit's flow.

8. Sunscreen.

Though unnoticed at the time, the sun's influence becomes obviously apparent when we find freckles, tan lines, and sunburn. We may not see the Spirit's hand in our lives until the evidence becomes clear later on, but that doesn't mean He's not by our sides all along the way.

9. A ribbon.

A gift is a gift is a gift, but a gift that's been tied with a ribbon is simply sublime. Your trinket for remembering God's spiritual gifts simply has to be a ribbon.

10. Seeds.

We all want to live fruitful lives which bring glory to God. Since this week's lesson has focused on fruit, our trinket this week will be the beginning of all fruitfulness—seeds. The Spirit has been implanted into our hearts, and the potential is there for a full and ripe harvest.

11. A pitcher.

Our spiritual life cannot flourish without the Spirit pouring through our lives. We need His filling, His permeation, His saturation. Our lives can brim over with the Spirit's influence.

12. A paint brush.

Just as a watercolorist is often surprised by the movement of water and paint across paper, we can be surprised by the Spirit's work in our hearts. Our life and His just kind of flow together, and we never really know what it'll become. All we can do is hang on to the promise that it'll be something beautiful.

What Shall We Study Next?

Women of Faith® has a series of study guides on various topics to help you draw closer to God.

Receiving God's Goodness

Imagine this. You're in a dungeon. Your cell is dark and dank. The floor is scattered with musty straw. Chains anchor you to the wall. There is no window—no glimpse of sky, no breath of fresh air. The only sounds you hear are the drip of condensation off bare stone and the rustle of rats. You crouch in the corner—listless, hopeless, defeated. Then you hear something unexpected. The crash of a distant door, the clamor of running feet. A key scrapes in the door to your cell, and the door swings open. There stands a rescuer, a knight in shining armor. He bends down, removes your chains, and lifts you to your feet. "Come, let's get you out of here." But you pull away and back against the wall. "There must be some mistake. You must be looking for some other prisoner." With a tilt of the head, He asks, "And why do you think that?" Shrugging, you reply, "Well, because I committed a crime. I'm guilty. I deserve to be here. You should be looking for someone who is innocent and doesn't belong here at all." With a nod of understanding, He takes your hand, "I know all that, but it's you I've come for. Don't you want to be free? I have come to set you free."

Unexpected mercy. God, in His goodness, sent Jesus to set the captives free. We were guilty, deserving of death, and living without hope when the door swung open. Unmerited favor. Jesus made it possible for our crimes to be forgiven, for our guilty verdict to be overturned, for our record to be wiped clean. Grace. The happy ending we didn't deserve.

CONTAGIOUS JOY

"A twinkle in the eye means joy in the heart." –Proverbs 15:30 MSG

You're walking down the street on a dreary, drizzly day. Everything is gray and gloomy, damp and disheartening. Shoulders hunched against the wet, you slog ahead in a dismal funk. Then, something catches your interest. Your ears pick up the sound of a cheerful whistle just ahead. To your astonishment, you're confronted with a woman in a luminescent yellow raincoat and bright green galoshes toting a polka-dot umbrella. Her spirits are obviously undampened by the inclement weather. In fact, she appears to be dancing to her own tune right between the raindrops. Suddenly, she takes a mighty leap, landing in a particularly large puddle and making a satisfying ker-splash. A smile tugs at your own lips. You can't help it. This gal's joy is contagious!

Joy has a way of working its way from the inside out. When our lives are filled with joy, we turn heads, too! The symptoms are unmistakable. A twinkle in the eye. A ready smile. A skip in the step. A song in the heart. Joy lends a glow to the face and a lilt to the voice. Joyful people whistle while they work and break into spontaneous song. And joy is contagious. So what about you? Would you be diagnosed as a puddle plodder, or a puddle jumper?

Yearning for a more joyful outlook on life? Joy is the birthright of every believer, but rainy days have a way of distracting us from that fact. In this study, we'll take a careful look at this uniquely Christian characteristic. We have every reason to be joyful. We can express our inner joy in numerous ways. We can even hang onto joy when other emotions clamor through our hearts. Joy can have the effect of effervescence, exuberance, exhilaration and enthusiasm. Joy is our strength and our song. It provides a solid foundation in our hearts. And although joy isn't exactly the same as happiness or glee, it leads conveniently into them. Joy is infectious, transmittable, spreadable, and catching. In a word, joy is contagious!

LEADER'S GUIDE

Chapter 1

1. "Behold, God is great, and we do not know Him; Nor can the number of His years be discovered" (Job 36:26 NKJV). God is so very great that we can't ever really comprehend Him. He's beyond knowing. Our minds cannot even grasp the vastness of eternity, let alone the Creator of everything. Yet our mind-boggling God invites us to walk what trails we can, and know Him as much as we are able. We are invited to search the unsearchable and know the unknowable.

2. "That you may know that there is no one like the Lord our God" (Ex. 8:10 NKJV). "That you may know that the Lord Himself is God; there is none other besides Him" (Deut. 4:35 NKJV). "Therefore know this day, and consider it in your heart, that the Lord Himself is God in heaven above and on the earth beneath; there is no other" (Deut. 4:39 NKJV). "Be still, and know that I am God; I will be exalted among the nations, I will be exalted in the earth" (Ps. 46:10 NKJV). "Know that the Lord, He is God; it is He who made us, and not we ourselves" (Ps. 100:3 NKJV).

3. "Then I will give them a heart to know Me, that I am the Lord; and they shall be My people, and I will be their God" (Jer. 24:7 NKJV). It's no wonder that there is a longing in our hearts to be close to God and to know Him better. That longing for spiritual intimacy in us is a gift from God Himself. He wants us to want to know Him.

4. "We know that we are of God, and the whole world lies under the sway of the wicked one. And we know that the Son of God has come and has given us an understanding, that we may know Him who is true; and we are in Him who is true, in His Son Jesus Christ. This is the true God and eternal life" (1 John 5:19–20 NKJV). We are of God. Jesus came so that we could have understanding. He came so we could know God. Another versions says, "We know that the Son of God has come, and he has given us understanding so that we can know the true God" (1 John 5:20 NLT). Without Jesus, we could never have known God.

5. "God has revealed them to us through His Spirit. For the Spirit searches all things, yes, the deep things of God" (1 Cor. 2:10 NKJV). The Spirit is the key. He searches out the things we need to and long to know, then teaches them to us. Think about this! God revealed Himself to men through the Spirit, then the Spirit moved those men to write those things down for us. That is how we came to have the Scriptures!

6. "For what man knows the things of a man except the spirit of the man which is in him? Even so no one knows the things of God except the Spirit of God. Now we have received, not the spirit of the world, but the Spirit who is from God, that we might know the things that have been freely given to us by God" (1 Cor. 2:11–12 NKJV). It is through the Spirit that we can know what God has given to us. He teaches us, helps us to understand, and assures us that we are God's. The Spirit helps us to know the riches that are ours by God's gift to us.

7. God may be unchanging, but because we don't know everything about Him, He still surprises us. Circumstances often force us to adjust our perceptions of who God is and what He is doing. Spiritual intimacy often drops us down in the middle of strange places in our hearts. But the Holy Spirit is the one who helps us get our bearings. Even if our whole world seems to turn upside down, some things we can always know to be true. The Spirit unerringly points us toward these truths and steadies our faith.

8. "They seek Me daily, And delight to know My ways, As a nation that did righteousness, And did not forsake the ordinance of their God. They ask of Me the ordinances of justice; They take delight in approaching God" (Is. 58:2 NKJV). What a beautiful description of a people who long to know God. A lifelong journey must be taken one day at a time. This verse talks about seeking God daily, and never losing the delight of doing so.

9. "Let him who glories glory in this, That he understands and knows Me, That I am the Lord, exercising lovingkindness, judgment, and righteousness in the earth. For in these I delight" (Jer. 9:24 NKJV). The crowning achievement of our lives should be wrapped up in our knowing God. We need to know Him, understand Him, trust Him. This is a part of spiritual intimacy. But there are two sides to every relationship. We can know God, but it doesn't stop there. He knows us intimately!

Chapter 2

1. "For He knows the secrets of the heart" (Ps. 44:21 NKJV). God knows our hearts. He knows the secrets that hide there. He knows our thoughts, our feelings, our impulses, our longings. He knows us better than we know ourselves!

2. "The Lord does not see as man sees; for man looks at the outward appearance, but the Lord looks at the heart" (1 Sam. 16:7 NKJV). We can't fool God, for He always sees right to the heart of a matter. But on the flip side, vulnerability with God is no problem. He already knows it all, and we know He loves us anyhow.

3. "The Spirit of God has made me, And the breath of the Almighty gives me life" (Job 33:4 NKJV). When we think of God as Creator, we generally think back to the Garden of Eden and Adam and Eve. But we would do well to remember that God made each and every one of us. He knew what color eyes we would have, how many hairs would be on our head, and what our favorite food would be. He gave us our personality, making it unique. He gave us talents and abilities. And then He gave us life. "The breath of the Almighty gives me life."

4. "Your hands have made me and fashioned me, An intricate unity" (Job 10:8 NKJV). Have you ever felt the pride and love that comes from making something with your own hands? Is it any wonder that God cares so much for us? He knows us so well because He's made us—right down to the intricacies! We are His own handiwork.

5. "For You **formed** my **inward parts**; You **covered** me in my mother's womb. I will praise You, for I am **fearfully** and **wonderfully** made; Marvelous are Your works, And that my soul knows very well. My **frame** was not **hidden** from You, When I was made in **secret**, And **skillfully** wrought in the lowest parts of the earth. Your eyes saw my **substance**, being yet **unformed**. And in Your book they all were written, The days **fashioned** for me, When as yet there were none of them" (Ps. 139: 13–16 NKJV).

6. "For we are His workmanship" (NKJV). "We are God's masterpiece" (NLT). There's nothing accidental or haphazard about us. The person of the heart, the person that we are inside, is a precious masterpiece of God's own making.

7. "Now what more can David say to You? For You, Lord God, know Your servant" (2 Sam. 7:20 NKJV). We can't tell God anything He doesn't already know about ourselves, but that doesn't mean He doesn't want us to tell Him about what we're thinking or feeling. "Before they call, I will answer; And while they are still speaking, I will hear" (Is. 65:24 NKJV). Our prayers connect us to God. They are our most intimate form of communication.

8. "O God, You know my foolishness; And my sins are not hidden from You" (Ps. 69:5 NKJV). "The Lord knows the thoughts of man, That they are futile" (Ps. 94:11 NKJV). "Search me, O God, and know my heart; Try me, and know my anxieties" (Ps. 139:23 NKJV). We are known. Every good bit, every bad bit. The Lord knows our hopes and dreams, our doubts and fears.

9. "The love of God has been poured out in our hearts by the Holy Spirit who was given to us" (Rom. 5:5 NKJV). The Holy Spirit's presence in our lives is just one proof of God's great love for us. In the next lesson, we'll talk even more about the Spirit.

Chapter 3

1. "I indeed baptized you with water, but He will baptize you with the Holy Spirit" (Mark 1:8 NKJV). John the Baptizer told those who were following him that when Jesus the Messiah came, He would do something far greater. Though John baptized with water in the Jordan River, Jesus would be able to baptize believers with the Holy Spirit.

2. "Nevertheless I tell you the truth. It is to your advantage that I go away; for if I do not go away, the Helper will not come to you; but if I depart, I will send Him to you" (John 16:7 NKJV). Jesus told His dear friends that it would be to their advantage that He leave. This must have confounded His disciples. But Jesus said that unless He left, the Spirit could not be sent. When Jesus returned to His Father, He could send the Helper to them.

3. "When the Helper comes, whom I shall send to you from the Father, the Spirit of truth who proceeds from the Father, He will testify of Me" (John 15:26 NKJV). One of the Helper's purposes in our lives was to testify to the believer about Jesus.

4. "When He, the Spirit of truth, has come, He will guide you into all truth; for He will not speak on His own authority, but whatever He hears He will speak; and He will tell you things to come" (John 16:13 NKJV). The Spirit is able to guide us toward the truth. He lets us know what God wants us to know—prompting, enlightening, urging, and convicting.

5. "The Helper, the Holy Spirit, whom the Father will send in My name, He will teach you all things, and bring to your remembrance all things that I said to you" (John 14:26 NKJV). During those early day s of the Church, the Spirit enabled each of the disciples to remember every thing that Jesus had taught them over their years together. Today, the Spirit still helps us to recall the words of Christ and the Word. He brings to mind those Scriptures we have committed to memory.

6. "And I will pray the Father, and He will give you another Helper, that He may abide with you forever" (John 14:16 NKJV). Jesus promised that the Helper will abide with us forever!

7. "Behold, God is my helper; The Lord is with those who uphold my life" (Ps. 54:4 NKJV). God Himself is our helper. It is one of His own titles. We should never be ashamed or affronted to take up the role of helpers.

8. "So we may boldly say: 'The Lord is my helper; I will not fear. What can man do to me?'" (Heb. 13:6 NKJV). God is our ever present help in time of need! We need never fear, because the Lord is our helper. This fact alone makes the writer of Hebrews encourage us to boldness.

9. "The Holy Spirit whom God has given to those who obey Him" (Acts 5:32 NKJV). When we are obedient to the Lord—believing Jesus and belonging to God—we are given the gift of the Holy Spirit. "Partakers of the Holy Spirit" (Heb. 6:4 NKJV). Every believer is a partaker of the Spirit. We each have Him residing in our hearts. What an amazing thought!

Chapter 4

1. "They shall call His name Immanuel, which is translated, 'God with us'" (Matt. 1:23 NKJV). It was in His very name. Jesus Himself was God with us! He left heaven's glories to be a man. He walked among the people, showed them God's love, and spoke to them the words of life.

2. "As You, Father, are in Me, and I in You; that they also may be one in Us" (John 17:21 NKJV). Not only was Jesus "God with us." He was one with God and offered us a way to be one with Him. "God with us" offered us a way to be with God!

3. "That Christ may dwell in your hearts through faith" (Eph. 3:17 NKJV). When we speak to children, we often say that salvation is inviting Jesus into our hearts. This is the verse from which we get this idea.

4. "You are not in the flesh but in the Spirit, if indeed the Spirit of God dwells in you. Now if anyone does not have the Spirit of Christ, he is not His" (Rom. 8:9 NKJV). Paul lets us know that we have the Spirit of God, also called the Spirit of Christ, dwelling in our hearts. In fact, Paul indicates that the presence of this Spirit is the proof of salvation, for only those who belong to God have Him!

5. "Do you not know that you are the temple of God and that the Spirit of God dwells in you?" (1 Cor. 3:16 NKJV). Paul says we are temples—the dwelling place of God. Set apart, sacred, made holy by the One who lives within.

6. "Or do you not know that your body is the temple of the Holy Spirit who is in you, whom you have from God, and you are not your own?" (1 Cor. 6:19 NKJV). Paul states again that our bodies serve as a temple for the Holy Spirit. He's in us, this One sent from God. But then Paul adds one surprising statement. We are not our own. Apparently, God's residency in our heart gives Him a "squatter's rights." Put simply, He owns us! We belong to Him.

7. God gave us the abilities and interests that make us who we are. He didn't give us these good things only to take them away from us in some kind of hostile takeover. We need to look carefully at how the Lord put us together, for He did so with a purpose. Each of us is uniquely made to fulfill some part in God's overall plan. With the Spirit's help, we can find the way we were made to bring glory to God's name, not our own.

8. "In whom you also are being built together for a dwelling place of God in the Spirit" (Eph. 2:22 NKJV). We aren't just a bunch of little temples for the Spirit to dwell in. We are being built together as one dwelling. The corporate Church is a dwelling place for God's Spirit as well.

9. "The whole body, joined and knit together by what every joint supplies, according to the effective working by which every part does its share, causes growth of the body for the edifying of itself in love" (Eph. 4:16 NKJV). We are called the body of Christ, and in this verse Paul describes the proper working of each member to the joining of knitting. As we each do our share and edify each other in love, we're woven more tightly together and we grow. This happens when the Spirit is able to work in and through our lives.

Chapter 5

1. "In the name of the Father and of the Son and of the Holy Spirit" (Matt. 28:19 NKJV). Here are the three mentioned together. The Father is considered the First Person of the Trinity, the Son the Second, and the Holy Spirit the Third Person.

2. This is indeed an early mention! "The earth was without form, and void; and darkness was on the face of the deep. And the Spirit of God was hovering over the face of the waters" (Gen. 1:2 NKJV). God's Spirit was at work right from the beginning!

3. "The Holy Spirit will come upon you, and the power of the Highest will over-shadow you; therefore, also, that Holy One who is to be born will be called the Son of God" (Luke 1:35 NKJV). "Do not be afraid to take to you Mary your wife, for that which is conceived in her is of the Holy Spirit" (Matt. 1:20 NKJV). The Spirit is the One who brought about Mary's immaculate conception. The Third Person of the Trinity made the virgin birth a reality.

4. "And the Holy Spirit descended in bodily form like a dove upon Him, and a voice came from heaven which said, 'You are My beloved Son; in You I am well pleased'" (Luke 3:22 NKJV). Here we see the Three Persons of the Trinity together again. Jesus is being baptized, the Spirit descends upon Him like a dove, and the Father speaks from Heaven, declaring His pleasure.

5. "For there are three that bear witness in heaven: the Father, the Word, and the Holy Spirit; and these three are one" (1 John 5:7 NKJV). As you may know, Jesus is often referred to in John's writings as the Word. So here we have the three persons of the Trinity mentioned together again: The Father, the Word (Jesus), and the Spirit.

6. d, f, a, e, b, c

7. "It is the Spirit who bears witness, because the Spirit is truth" (1 John 5:6 NKJV). John tells us that the Spirit is truth. This is not so surprising. Jesus Himself told us He was the way, the truth and the life. If Jesus was the truth, then it makes sense that the Spirit (also God) was truth as well.

8. It is very interesting to compare translations, so let's look at a few. "It is the Spirit who gives life…The words that I speak to you are spirit, and they are life" (John 6:63 NKJV). "It is the Spirit who gives eternal life. Human effort accomplishes nothing" (NLT). "The Spirit can make life. Sheer muscle and willpower don't make anything happen. Every word I've spoken to you is a Spirit-word, and so it is life-making" (MSG). The Spirit gives us life.

9. "For what man knows the things of a man except the spirit of the man which is in him? Even so no one knows the things of God except the Spirit of God" (1 Cor. 2:11 NKJV). "No one can know what anyone else is really thinking except that person alone, and no one can know God's thoughts except God's own Spirit" (NLT). Who could know God better than God? If we want to know God intimately, we must learn about Him through the Spirit. The Spirit's presence in our hearts is so vital because it is through Him that we touch God's thoughts.

Chapter 6

1. "Most assuredly, I say to you, unless one is born of water and the Spirit, he cannot enter the kingdom of God" (John 3:5 NKJV). "That which is born of the flesh is flesh, and that which is born of the Spirit is spirit" (John 3:6 NKJV).

2. "But you were washed, but you were sanctified, but you were justified in the name of the Lord Jesus and by the Spirit of our God" (1 Cor. 6:11 NKJV). Washed! The Spirit does the work of cleansing our hearts of sin. Sanctified! The Spirit sets us apart and makes us holy in God's sight. Justified! The Spirit declares us righteous because Jesus is righteous.

3. "Who also has sealed us and given us the Spirit in our hearts as a guarantee" (2 Cor. 1:22 NKJV). "He who has prepared us for this very thing is God, who also has given us the Spirit as a guarantee" (2 Cor. 5:5 NKJV). In both of these verses, Paul says that the Spirit is in our hearts as a guarantee. He was given to us like a deposit, or earnest money, or a down payment against what we will have entirely later on.

4. "In Him you also trusted, after you heard the word of truth, the gospel of your salvation; in whom also, having believed, you were sealed with the Holy Spirit of promise" (Eph. 1:13 NKJV). We were sealed by the Spirit when we were saved.

5. "The Holy Spirit of God, by whom you were sealed for the day of redemption" (Eph. 4:30 NKJV). We have a great future, a divine inheritance, an eternal reward ahead of us. The Spirit seals us for the day when we receive it all. He's our guarantee that God's many promises will belong to us one day.

6. "Who is the guarantee of our inheritance until the redemption of the purchased possession, to the praise of His glory" (Eph. 1:14 NKJV). The Spirit in our hearts reassures us of our place in God's heart and of the sureness of God's promises. He gives us confidence that our inheritance is real and ready for us in heaven.

7. b, d, a, e, c

8. "Do not cast me away from Your presence, And do not take Your Holy Spirit from me" (Ps. 51:11 NKJV). Often we don't appreciate a thing until it's been taken away from us. We grow accustomed to it, and begin to take it for granted. David didn't take the Lord's Spirit for granted, but rather included words of thanksgiving and love for Him in his psalms.

9. "Nevertheless the solid foundation of God stands, having this seal: 'The Lord knows those who are His'" (2 Tim. 2:19 NKJV). We are His. He has sealed us. It's just as if we were touched by His divine finger, and He said, "This one's mine!"

Chapter 7

1. "You shall receive power when the Holy Spirit has come upon you" (Acts 1:8 NKJV). Jesus had been preparing His disciples all along the way for the goodbye that had to come. But Jesus consistently encouraged His friends that they would not be left alone. The Comforter would come, and He would come with power.

2. "And suddenly there came a sound from heaven, as of a rushing mighty wind, and it filled the whole house where they were sitting. Then there appeared to them divided tongues, as of fire, and one sat upon each of them. And they were all filled with the Holy Spirit" (Acts 2:2–4 NKJV). A mighty rushing wind!

3. "God anointed Jesus of Nazareth with the Holy Spirit and with power" (Acts 10:38 NKJV). The Spirit and power go hand in hand throughout the New Testament.

4. "My speech and my preaching were not with persuasive words of human wisdom, but in demonstration of the Spirit and of power" (1 Cor. 2:4 NKJV). The Spirit is most often associate with words. Whenever you find a man or woman filled with the Spirit, they will usually be given the boldness to speak. "For our gospel did not come to you in word only, but also in power, and in the Holy Spirit and in much assurance" (1 Thess. 1:5 NKJV). Words. The very words of the gospel. God's Words were given by the power of the Spirit. "But truly I am full of power by the Spirit of the Lord, And of justice and might, To declare to Jacob his transgression And to Israel his sin" (Micah 3:8 NKJV). The Spirit gave the prophet the power to speak, even when the message may have been an unwelcome one.

5. "The Spirit of the Lord God is upon Me, Because the Lord has anointed Me To preach good tidings to the poor; He has sent Me to heal the brokenhearted, To proclaim liberty to the captives, And the opening of the prison to those who are bound" (Is. 61:1 NKJV). Here is a wonderful example of what someone can do when they are empowered by the Spirit for God's work! Incidentally, this prophecy was fulfilled by Jesus, and we actually find these words quoted in Luke 4:18.

6. "Now when they came up out of the water, the Spirit of the Lord caught Philip away, so that the eunuch saw him no more; and he went on his way rejoicing" (Acts 8:39 NKJV). Wow! One minute Philip was there, and the next he was gone. God's power can do miraculous things.

7. "In mighty signs and wonders, by the power of the Spirit of God" (Rom. 15:19 NKJV). Paul was always careful to point out that the wonders people witnessed in his presence were by God's power and not his own. Often these miracles opened up the doors so that the gospel could be preached.

8. "'Not by might nor by power, but by My Spirit,' Says the Lord of hosts" (Zech. 4:6 NKJV). Too often we try to accomplish things in our own strength. We work hard. We achieve. We accomplish. And then we take the credit. In this verse we are reminded that God's work is done in God's power by God's Spirit. Our own efforts, no matter how well-intentioned, are not enough.

9. "For God has not given us a spirit of fear, but of power and of love and of a sound mind" (2 Tim. 1:7 NKJV). God's Spirit has been given to us, and it brings with it power.

Chapter 8

1. "Who has directed the Spirit of the Lord, Or as His counselor has taught Him?" (Is. 40:13 NKJV). The answer, of course, is no one. But consider the question more closely. What is Isaiah asking? Can anyone direct God's Spirit—influence Him, persuade Him, order Him around? No. And can anyone set themselves up as the Spirit's counselor—advising Him, influencing Him, teaching Him something new? Again, no!

2. "Then Jesus, being filled with the Holy Spirit, returned from the Jordan and was led by the Spirit into the wilderness" (Luke 4:1 NKJV). Jesus was filled with the Spirit and allowed the Spirit to direct His decisions and His actions. He followed the Spirit's lead. "For I know that this will turn out for my deliverance through your prayer and the supply of the Spirit of Jesus Christ" (Phil. 1:19 NKJV). Paul was confident that everything would turn out all right because he trusted the Spirit to supply what was needed.

3. "As they ministered to the Lord and fasted, the Holy Spirit said, 'Now separate to Me Barnabas and Saul for the work to which I have called them.'... So being sent out by the Holy spirit, they went down" (Acts 13:2, 4 NKJV). The Spirit spoke! He gave specific direction. He called workers. And He sent them out.

4. "When they arrest you and deliver you up, do not worry beforehand, or pre-meditate what you will speak. But whatever is given you in that house, speak that; for it is not you who speak, but the Holy Spirit" (Mark 13:11 NKJV). "For the Holy spirit will teach you in that very hour what you ought to say" (Luke 12:12 NKJV).

5. "The Spirit of the Lord spoke by me, And His word was on my tongue" (2 Sam. 23:2 NKJV). There are times when I say just the right thing, or turn a phrase just so, and I stop and wonder, "Where did that come from?" The Spirit influenced the prophets of old. He inspired the writers of Scripture. Even today He uses His quiet influence, inspiring us with good words.

6. "Walking in the fear of the Lord and in the comfort of the Holy Spirit" (Acts 9:31 NKJV). The Spirit comforts us, which makes sense when you recall that He is called the Comforter. He comes alongside us and helps us in our spiritual walk. "If there is any consolation in Christ, if any comfort of love, if any fellowship of the Spirit" (Phil. 2:1 NKJV). The Spirit encourages fellowship in the Body of Christ. He uses His influence to strengthen the good and necessary bonds of love and friendship within the church. Think about it—we all share the same Spirit!

7. "You, beloved, **building** yourselves up on your most holy **faith**, **praying** in the **Holy Spirit**" (Jude 1:20 NKJV). "I will **pray** with the **spirit**, and I will also **pray** with the **understanding**. I will **sing** with the **spirit**, and I will also **sing** with the **under-standing**" (1 Cor. 14:15 NKJV). "**Praying** always with all **prayer** and **supplication** in the **Spirit**" (Eph. 6:18 NKJV).

8. "Likewise the Spirit also helps in our weaknesses. For we do not know what we should pray for as we ought, but the Spirit Himself makes intercession for us with groanings which cannot be uttered" (Rom. 8:26 NKJV). The Spirit's quiet influence shows up in our prayer lives. We don't always know what to say to God when we come to Him in prayer. But the Spirit who knows us so intimately knows just what our hearts long to say. He helps us to pray.

9. "And after the earthquake a fire, but the Lord was not in the fire; and after the fire a still small voice" (1 Kings 19:12 NKJV). Sometimes the Spirit is a rushing wind, but more often His influence is that of the still small voice, quietly influencing our spir-itual walk with God.

Chapter 9

1. "When He ascended on high, He led captivity captive, And gave gifts to men" (Eph. 4:8 NKJV). After Jesus departed, He sent gifts to His followers—parting gifts. These included the Holy Spirit Himself, but also those things we now refer to as spiritual gifts.

2. "Repent, and let every one of you be baptized in the name of Jesus Christ for the remission of sins; and you shall receive the gift of the Holy Spirit" (Acts 2:38 NKJV). It's good to remember that the Spirit Himself is a gift. We receive Him when we are saved.

3. "If you then, being evil, know how to give good gifts to your children, how much more will your Father who is in heaven give good things to those who ask Him!" (Matt. 7:11 NKJV). God's gifts are good ones.

4. "Every good gift and every perfect gift is from above, and comes down from the Father of lights, with whom there is no variation or shadow of turning" (James 1:17 NKJV). Not only does God give good gifts, but every good gift comes ultimately from His hand! This would, of course, include our spiritual gifts.

5. "For the gifts and the calling of God are irrevocable" (Rom. 11:29 NKJV). Whether we realize it or not, our spiritual gifts are there. They may lie dormant for a season, or take decades to mature, but they're there. God doesn't threaten us to use them or lose them. Even in this, God is gracious. We may not discover a gift we've had for years, only to be surprised by the latest twist in God's delightful path for our lives.

6. "There are diversities of gifts, but the same Spirit" (1 Cor. 12:4 NKJV). The combinations of gifts in each of us is as varied as the individuals that have them. But just as we each have our own special place and purpose in God's plan, so each of us has been uniquely gifted and empowered to do our thing.

7. "Having then gifts differing according to the grace that is given to us, let us use them" (Rom. 12:6 NKJV). You've got gifts? Then use them! Spiritual gifts were never meant to sit in a curio cabinet and be admired. They were always and ever intended to be put to good, hard use! I can't say it enough—spiritual gifts are practical gifts.

8. "Earnestly desire the best gifts" (1 Cor. 12:31 NKJV). "Pursue love, and desire spiritual gifts" (1 Cor. 14:1 NKJV). We should desire them—want to possess them. But keep in mind that Paul wasn't collecting them like bottle caps. Paul's prayer was that

God would equip him to do the work of the ministry. He wanted to be counted worthy to serve.

9. "Even so you, since you are zealous for spiritual gifts, let it be for the edification of the church that you seek to excel" (1 Cor. 14:12 NKJV). We don't desire gifts to be able to claim we have them. They're not badges we can boast about or something to bulk up our spiritual resumes. Paul says if you want to be zealous for the gifts, make sure it's for the right reasons. For God's purpose in giving them is for the edification of the church—building it up, strengthening and encouraging.

Chapter 10

1. "Even so, every **good** tree **bears good** fruit, but a **bad** tree **bears bad** fruit. A **good** tree cannot **bear bad** fruit, nor can a **bad tree** bear **good** fruit" (Matt. 7:17–18 NKJV). "Either make the **tree good** and its **fruit good**, or else make the **tree bad** and its **fruit bad**; for a **tree** is **known** by its **fruit**" (Matt. 12:33 NKJV). "For every **tree** is **known** by its own **fruit**. For men do not gather **figs** from **thorns**, nor do they gather **grapes** from a **bramble bush**" (Luke 6:44 NKJV).

2. "Now the ones that fell among thorns are those who, when they have heard, go out and are choked with cares, riches, and pleasures of life, and bring no fruit to maturity" (Luke 8:14 NKJV). Life is filled with little distractions. When we are caught up in our day-to-day activities, it's far too easy to push our spiritual life onto the back burner. Then we don't grow, and we don't bear any fruit.

3. "But the ones that fell on the good ground are those who, having heard the word with a noble and good heart, keep it and bear fruit with patience" (Luke 8:15 NKJV). In this verse we find a simple little list of the qualities that characterize a heart that's ready to flourish—listening, noble, good, patient. What's more, this verse says that these people both hear the word and keep it. That means following through, doing the right thing, and putting into practice what we know we should.

4. "Sow for yourselves righteousness; Reap in mercy; Break up your fallow ground, For it is time to seek the Lord, Till He comes and rains righteousness on you" (Hosea 10:12 NKJV). This is a beautifully expressive verse. The command is to sow righteousness. In order to do so, we may need to break up our fallow ground—ground that's lain unused for a long time.

5. "Every branch in Me that does not bear fruit He takes away; and every branch that bears fruit He prunes, that it may bear more fruit" (John 15:2 NKJV). Sometimes in order for fruit to grow, pruning has to take place. Those things that hamper our spiritual lives must be sheered away. "Now no chastening seems to be joyful for the present, but painful; nevertheless, afterward it yields the peaceable fruit of righteousness to those who have been trained by it" (Heb. 12:11 NKJV). Pruning and chastening appear to work wonders in our lives, whether we appreciate them or not. The writer of Hebrews tells us that the training isn't nice to go through, but the end result is worth it. "Abide in Me, and I in you. As the branch cannot bear fruit of itself, unless it abides in the vine, neither can you, unless you abide in Me" (John 15:4 NKJV). We cannot bear fruit by a sheer act of our will. All the good intentions and perseverance in the world doesn't bring good fruit. Fruit only grows in a life that depends on the Lord. Only those who abide in Him will bear any fruit to maturity. "I am the vine, you are the branches. He who abides in Me, and I in him, bears much fruit; for without Me you can do nothing" (John 15:5 NKJV). Those who abide in Jesus are fruitful. Those who do not can do nothing. Life in Christ is an all or nothing commitment!

6. "You did not choose Me, but I chose you and appointed you that you should go and bear fruit, and that your fruit should remain" (John 15:16 NKJV). You can not get more direct than this—I chose you so that you could bear fruit. Our lives should be characterized by fruit as well—fruit that will remain and flourish long after we're gone.

7. "By this My Father is glorified, that you bear much fruit" (John 15:8 NKJV). When we bear fruit, we bring Glory to God.

8. "**Walk** in the Spirit" (Gal. 5:16 NKJV). "**Led** by the Spirit" (Gal. 5:18 NKJV). "**Live** in the Spirit" (Gal. 5:25 NKJV).

9. "The fruit of the Spirit is love, joy, peace, longsuffering, kindness, goodness, faithfulness, gentleness, self-control" (Gal. 5:22–23 NKJV). "For the fruit of the Spirit is in all goodness, righteousness, and truth" (Eph. 5:9 NKJV). These are all good things, and as Paul says, "Against such there is no law" (Gal. 5:23 NKJV).

Chapter 11

1. "I will pour water on him who is thirsty, And floods on the dry ground; I will pour My Spirit on your descendants, And My blessing on your offspring" (Is. 44:3 NKJV). God promised to pour out His Spirit on His people. "Therefore being exalted to the right hand of God, and having received from the Father the promise of the Holy Spirit, He poured out this which you now see and hear" (Acts 2:33 NKJV). Jesus returned to the Father so that the promise of the Holy Spirit could be poured out on all believers. "And it shall come to pass afterward That I will pour out My Spirit on all flesh; Your sons and your daughters shall prophesy, Your old men shall dream dreams, Your young men shall see visions. And also on My menservants and on My maidservants I will pour out My Spirit in those days" (Joel 2:28–29 NKJV). God's promise of pouring out His spirit saw its first fulfillment in the lives of the 120 believers gathered together in the upper room at Pentecost.

2. "'Try Me now in this,' Says the Lord of hosts, 'If I will not open for you the windows of heaven And pour out for you such blessing That there will not be room enough to receive it'" (Mal. 3:10 NKJV). God's pouring is a promise to send blessings so abundant that we cannot possibly contain them all. We are filled to overflowing.

3. "My cup **runs over**" (Ps. 23:5 NKJV). "God does not **give** the **Spirit** by **measure**" (John 3:34 NKJV). "I have come that they may have **life**, and that they may have it **more abundantly**" (John 10:10 NKJV). "God is able to make **all** grace **abound** toward you, that you, always having **all sufficiency** in **all** things, may have an **abundance** for every good work" (2 Cor. 9:8 NKJV). "Now to Him who is able to do **exceedingly abundantly above** all that we **ask** or **think**, according to the power that works in us" (Eph. 3:20 NKJV). "Whom He **poured out** on us **abundantly** through Jesus Christ our Savior" (Titus 3:6 NKJV).

4. "Do not be drunk with wine, in which is dissipation; but be filled with the Spirit" (Eph. 5:18 NKJV). This is an interesting comparison and contrast. When someone is DUI (driving under the influence), everything they think or do is influenced by the alcohol that fills them. We aren't filled by the Spirit once we perform some rite or routine. The Spirit fills us when we bend to His influence and follow His lead. We are to be filled with the Spirit, living under His influence. The Spirit should guide our thoughts and steps, our attitudes and our actions.

5. "Being filled with the fruits of righteousness which are by Jesus Christ, to the glory and praise of God" (Phil. 1:11 NKJV). "We … do not cease to pray for you, and to ask that you may be filled with the knowledge of His will in all wisdom and spiritual understanding" (Col. 1:9 NKJV). The Spirit's filling of our lives plays out in practical ways. Not only are we blessed by God's abundance, but we are able to see results. Our lives are filled with good spiritual fruit, which brings glory and praise to God. Also, we are filled with understanding and can discern God's place and plan for us.

6. **Psalm 107:9** – God fills the hungry soul with goodness. **Psalm 126:2** – Our mouths are filled with laughter and singing. **Habakkuk 2:14** – The earth will be filled with the glory of the Lord. **Matthew 5:6** – Those who hunger and thirst for it will be filled with righteousness. **John 15:11** – Jesus assures us that we can be filled with joy. **Acts 14:17** – God fills our hearts with food and gladness. **Romans 15:13** – The God of hope fills us with all joy and peace. **Romans 15:14** – We are full of goodness and knowledge. **James 3:17** – The wisdom we gain from God is full of mercy and good fruits.

7. "Listen to this, O Job; Stand still and consider the wondrous works of God" (Job 37:14 NKJV). Sometimes we need to stop everything else we're doing in order to bring our minds around to spiritual things. "When I consider Your heavens, the work of Your fingers, The moon and the stars, which You have ordained, What is man that You are mindful of him, And the son of man that You visit him?" (Ps. 8:3–4 NKJV). Stop and smell the roses—for God calls to our hearts through the wonders of His creation. When we pause to consider all He has done and can do, our hearts are drawn to worship Him. "Consider what I say, and may the Lord give you understanding in all things" (2 Tim. 2:7 NKJV). Considering God's Word, meditating on the Scriptures, considering the meaning of the Bible's message—these things take time and quiet contemplation. To do this, we need to stop and think.

8. "I remember the days of old; I meditate on all Your works; I muse on the work of Your hands" (Ps. 143:5 NKJV). Trying to figure out what you should meditate about? Take some time to consider the hand of God in your life so far. What has God done in the past? "I call to remembrance my song in the night; I meditate within my heart, And my spirit makes diligent search" (Ps. 77:6 NKJV). Meditation can come at quiet times—in the shower, on the commute, in bed before sleep comes. Then, we look for God's purposes for our day. "I will meditate on Your precepts, And contemplate Your ways" (Ps. 119:15 NKJV). When meditation pulls our thoughts into the future, let it be on God's Word and God's ways instead of on worries.

9. "This Book of the Law shall not depart from your mouth, but you shall meditate in it day and night, that you may observe to do according to all that is written in it. For then you will make your way prosperous, and then you will have good success" (Josh. 1:8 NKJV). It's sometimes difficult to separate God's varied influence in our lives—God's grace, Jesus' love, the Spirit's prompting, the Word's teaching. In our pursuit of spiritual filling, we can begin with God's Word. It is His message to us, His revelation of Himself, and His Spirit inside our hearts responds to it. The Spirit teaches us what God's Word means. He brings it back to our mind so that we can consider it later. As God's Word influences our life, we bring glory to God.

Chapter 12

1. We like to have step-by-step instructions for the projects we set out to do. We'd be more comfortable moving forward if we are sure the next step is the right one to take. But our walk with the Lord isn't a project, and each of us has such unique circumstances that there's no one "right" way to grow. We can be sure of God's Word and His promises to us, but every step we take forward is taken in faith. Can you think of specific examples of this in your own life?

2. If we want to live a life that is pleasing to God, we can find out what to do as we gain a more intimate understanding of the Lord. This means having a growing, deepening relationship with our Savior through the Spirit's working in our hearts.

3. In our pursuit of greater intimacy with the Lord, we discover just how much depends on Him—not us. He is our source. He is our strength. He brings the harvest of maturity forth in our lives. Yet we have a part too. Our relationship with the Lord is intimate and organic. In other words, our relationship is a living thing. It grows and changes and bears fruit.

4. We're always changing, always growing, always learning something new. Though we're reaching toward spiritual maturity, none of us has arrived. Our relationship with the Lord—how we see Him, what we're thankful for, our awareness of Him, our trust and faith—changes all the time. Looking back, we can see how our love for the Lord has evolved over time. Looking forward, we see areas in our lives where we want to grow and mature.

5. We should never take the Holy Spirit for granted. He's a gift we should treasure. He moves and breathes in our hearts. He's the most intimate part of our lives with God. He changes us from the inside out so that we are fit for the Lord. By His influence, it is possible for us to bring glory to God.

6. "I pray that from his glorious, unlimited resources he will give you mighty inner strength through his Holy Spirit" (Eph. 3:16 NLT). As we go forward in our search for greater spiritual intimacy, accept Paul's prayer for the strength the Spirit will give along the way. He helps us to know Him.

7. "But we all, with unveiled face, beholding as in a mirror the glory of the Lord, are being transformed into the same image from glory to glory, just as by the Spirit of the Lord" (2 Cor. 3:18 NKJV). What's going on in our hearts? Transformation! The Spirit is at work in our lives, changing us from the inside out. When we are aware of what the Lord wants to do in our hearts, we can be teachable as we participate in the growing up process.

8. "The amazing grace of the Master, Jesus Christ, the extravagant love of God, the intimate friendship of the Holy Spirit, be with all of you" (2 Cor. 13:14 MSG). Grace, love, and friendship. What more could we need?

9. "Now may the God of hope fill you with all joy and peace in believing, that you may abound in hope by the power of the Holy Spirit" (Rom. 15:13 NKJV). Hope, joy, peace, and power by the Holy Spirit.

THE COMPLETE WOMEN OF FAITH®
STUDY GUIDE SERIES

NELSON IMPACT

A Division of Thomas Nelson Publishers

Since 1798

The Nelson Impact Team is here to answer your questions and suggestions as to how we can create more resources that benefit you, your family, and your community.

Contact us at Impact@thomasnelson.com